THE DEFINIT TO TR

(INCLUDING FUNICULARS)
IN THE BRITISH ISLES

THIRD EDITION
(originally entitled The Millennium Guide)

by

DAVID VOICE

PUBLISHED BY ADAM GORDON

Also by David Voice:

How to Go Tramway and Tramway Modelling

London's Tramways Their History and How to Model Them

What Colour Was That Tram?

Tramway Modelling in 'OO' Gauge

More Tramway Modelling in 'OO' Gauge

The Illustrated History of Kidderminster and Stourport Electric Tramway (with Melvyn Thompson)

How to Go Tram and Tramway Modelling, 2nd Edition

The Millennium guide to Trams in the British Isles

The Definitive Guide to Trams in the British Isles, First Edition

Toy and Model Trams of the World, Volume 1; Toys, Die Casts and Souvenirs (with Gottfried Kuře)

Toy and Model Trams of the World, Volume 2; Plastic, White Metal and Brass Models and Kits (with Gottfried Kuře)

Next Stop Seaton! (with David Jay)

Copyright 2005: All rights to the text and photographs are reserved to David Voice

A catalogue entry for this book is available from the British Library

ISBN 1874422486

Publication no. 50

Third Edition published 2004 by Adam Gordon, Kintradwell Farmhouse, Brora, Sutherland KW9 6LU

Tel: 01408 622660

Printed by Launton Press, Bicester, Oxfordshire

Typesetting and design by Trevor Preece: trevor@epic.gb.com

Scanning by David Voice

CONTENTS

INTRODUCTION

When I wrote the initial guide in 1999 I had no idea that within a few years I would be compiling a third edition. Although trams, by their very nature, run on rails firmly fixed to the ground there has been an enormous amount of change in the last few years. The third edition records all the changes that have taken place since the publication of the previous edition and gives the current situation.

The format and style of the guide remains very much the same. At the request of many readers the information has been extended to include four additional features. A map of the British Isles indicates where each tramway/funicular/museum is, and the nearest other listed attractions to each entry are now given. These are to help those visiting different parts of the country to identify the nearest tram interest when visiting a locality. The gauge of the tramway/funicular has been identified more clearly. Finally a new section has been added to give details on private funiculars that can be seen from public areas.

As before there is the usual word of caution. Where a tramcar is shown as "awaiting restoration" it usually means that it is barely recognisable as a tram. Other than broad dimensions little information can be obtained from such trams.

For ease of reference, the book is divided into sections. The first describes all the operating public tramway systems and funiculars in the British Isles. Since the publication of the second edition two new tram systems have been built, in Dublin and Nottingham and, surprisingly, four new funiculars (two are in the second section).

The second section gives details on museums and heritage tramways. Having myself had difficulties finding some of the museums I have given as clear directions as I can on how to get to them. Each museum has a National Grid Reference (with the exception of the Republic of Ireland). These can be found on all Ordnance Survey maps and on the large road maps produced by the AA. For those travelling by car I have, where possible, used motorway junctions as starting points. Those travelling by public transport are recommended to contact the organisation or local public transport operators for the latest information prior to travelling.

The third section is a new one. This gives details of the private funiculars in the British Isles. For such an unusual mode of transport it is surprising that several have been constructed for private use only. It also includes closed funiculars where there are remains to be seen.

The fourth section is a listing of every preserved tramcar in the British Isles and every British tramcar preserved abroad. I have, as far as possible, indicated whether public access is available and what sort of condition the tramcar is in. This of course varies from the rotting pile of wood waiting for restoration to a fully restored and operating tramcar looking like new. Where the tramcars ran on more than one system then each system is listed. The current livery gives the location, all others refer you to the current (or intended restored) livery. Many trams are in private ownership and are not open to the public. Please respect this and do not trespass. Often the owners are happy to make arrangements for those with a genuine interest. So contact the owners first.

Although you may not find all of them in your high street magazine shop, there is a surprising number of tramway magazines currently being published. The Directory lists them, their frequency of publication and how to get hold of copies. Then the many tramway societies, both local and national, that cater for tramway enthusiasts are listed; there must be one not far from where you live.

The next section is devoted to displays of model trams and model tramway layouts open to the public. This is followed by a section on model tramway manufacturers and suppliers.

NOTE:

Every effort has been made to check the information given in this book for accuracy. However, the publisher and author have used information given in good faith and cannot accept responsibility for any errors that may be discovered or for any changes made by organisations listed in the book, particularly in the availability of tramcars, the movement of tramcars, changes to the opening dates or times of museums or the condition of exhibits.

If you wish to see a particular tramcar in a particular livery I strongly suggest that you check, before setting out, that the tram is at the location you are going to, that it is available to be seen and that it is in the livery you expect. Access to private areas of running tramways is prohibited unless prior permission has been gained by the undertaking (usually a lengthy process). Museums are very helpful to the tramway researcher and, if practical, will allow closer inspection of exhibits that is not usually afforded to the general public. However, prior permission should always be obtained and all instructions strictly followed.

Some of the locations are more difficult to get to by public transport. Given the numerous changes that happen to public transport these days, I recommend that those wishing to travel by train and bus should contact the museum in advance and get up to date information on access by public transport. Indeed anyone intending to travel significant distances is advised to check with the undertaking that it will be open and that what you want to see is available

ACKNOWLEDGEMENTS
Although my name appears as the author, a book like this relies entirely on the generous help of a multitude of people. To all those that I wrote to or telephoned and who all, without exception, gave freely of their time to answer my queries, I owe an immense debt of gratitude. They are too numerous to name, but they know

who they are and I thank everyone. I would particularly acknowledge the patience of my family as I shut myself away to write yet more about trams; to Alan Kirkman for answering a barrage of impossible questions instantly; to Adam Gordon for his enthusiastic support and invaluable help in the composition and checking of the book; to Trevor Preece for his artistry in the page design and layout; to David Cole, Mark Hows and Adam Winstanley for allowing me to use their photographs.

David Voice, December 2004

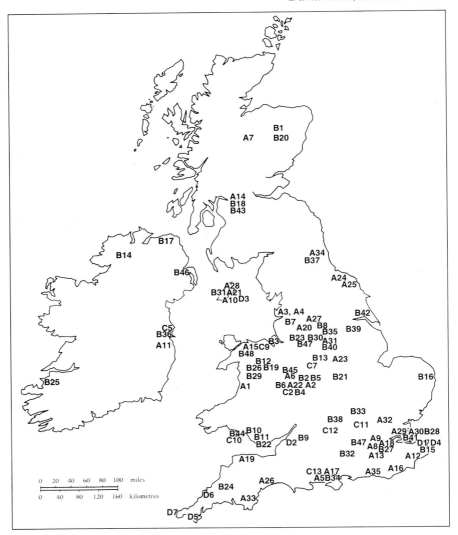

LIST OF ENTRIES

OPERATING PUBLIC TRAMWAYS AND FUNICULARS IN THE BRITISH ISLES

ABERYSTWYTH CLIFF RAILWAY

Address

Constitution Hill Ltd
Cliff Railway House
Cliff Terrace
Aberystwyth
Ceredigion
SY23 2DN

Tel: 01970 617642
GR: SN584826
Gauge: 4' 10"

Looking down the funicular with Cardigan Bay and Aberystwyth spread out below with the car "Lord Marks" ascending to the half way passing point.

Open

Daily from the middle of March to 5th November.

How to get there

By public transport: travel by rail to Aberystwyth Station. Ignoring the temptations of the Vale of Rheidol Railway, turn right out of the station to Alexandra Road, cross the road and slightly to the right is Terrace Road. Walk down Terrace Road to the sea front at Marine Terrace. Bear right and walk along the promenade to the end (Victoria Terrace). The cliff railway is on your right.

By car: enter Aberyswyth on either the A44 or the A487. Where they join head for the centre of the town along Northgate Street. Then instead of driving into the town centre, bear right into Queen's Road. The signs will show a cul de sac, but carry straight on. The cliff railway is directly ahead of you. Drive past it into Cliff Terrace. There is restricted on-street parking on this road. Otherwise head back to the town centre and use the car park in Bath Street.

Description

The cliff railway opened in 1896 using the water balance principle on two 4' 10" gauge tracks. It was converted to electric motor power in 1921. At 778ft, it now claims to be the longest electric cliff railway in Britain (the 'electric' being important as the Lynton water balance cliff railway is longer). Taken over by a community business (a "not for profit" organisation associated with Prospects, a national charity supporting adults with learning disabilities) in 1988, (along with all the other Constitution Hill facilities), there has been a programme of refurbishment and improvement. This is very welcome as the railway had been allowed to decline.

The full restoration of the area, including the camera obscura and Summerhouse Café, has been proceeding well. It is well worth a visit as the views from the top of the cliff railway are superb. The railway is unusual in naming its carriages after people associated with the railway, Lord Geraint and Lord Marks.

Tickets

Single or return tickets are available, purchased at the stations.

Nearby

Aberystwyth is rather isolated. The nearest other attraction is the funicular at the Centre for Alternative Technology at Machynlleth.

One of Britain's newest cable tramways, the Birmingham International Airport Skyrail, linking the airport with the railway station.

BIRMINGHAM INTERNATIONAL AIRPORT SKYRAIL

Address

Birmingham International Airport
Birmingham
B26 3QJ

Tel: 08707 335511
Web: www.bhx.co.uk
GR: SP180840
Gauge: Rubber tyres on concrete

Open
Daily all year.

How to get there
Public transport: Take a train to Birmingham International station. The Skyrail links the railway station with the airport.
By car: Leave the M42 at junction 6 (just south of the junction of the M6 and

M42). Follow the signs to Birmingham International Airport. Near the terminal buildings is plenty of short term parking (though expensive). Enter the International departures building (not the Eurohub). Go up a floor and Skyrail is on the east side.

Description

Officially opened on 7 March 2003, Skyrail is the new free link between Birmingham International Airport and the railway station. Originally the link was achieved by the Maglev, but this closed several years ago and travellers had to rely on a bus service. Now the old Maglev elevated concrete structure is used by Skyrail. There are two independent tracks each with a short articulated carriage. Each carriage is cable operated; the cable is continuous, running from the carriage to one end, round a pulley and back to the other end of the line, round the powered pulley and back to the carriage. This enables the power house at one end to move the carriages in either direction. The system is fully automated, 585 metres long, has a top speed of 22mph and takes 90 seconds to complete the journey. When you ride on it why not reflect that the ultra modern, magnetically levitated linear motor driven Maglev has been replaced by a cable operated system. This harks back to 1888 when Birmingham's cable tramway opened. It closed in 1911 and the city had to wait 92 years for another cable hauled transport system.

Tickets

Free.

Fleet

Two 2-section units, rubber tyred and guided by a monorail. No numbers.

Nearby

Aston Manor Road Transport Museum, Black Country Living Museum and the Birmingham and Midland Museum of Transport.

BLACKPOOL NORTH PIER TRAMWAY

Address

North Pier
Talbot Square
Blackpool

The tramcar has been removed and the tramway is now closed.

The Boat tramcar is a summer favourite. Here two are halted at Ash Street, Fleetwood.

BLACKPOOL TRAMWAY

Address

Blackpool Transport Services Limited
Rigby Road
Blackpool
FY1 5DD

Tel: 01253 473000
Web: www.blackpooltransport.com
GR: SD309351
Gauge: 4' 8½"

Open

All year.

How to get there

By public transport: travel by rail to Blackpool North station. From the station the promenade and tramway is about a ten-minute walk. Walk down Talbot Road to the promenade at Talbot Square and North Pier.

By car: From Junction 4 of the M55 carry on following signs to Blackpool. The depot is at Rigby Road, so exit the car parking area at signpost to Rigby Road.

Alternatively follow signs to South Shore and park at Starr Gate and take a tram.

Description

Blackpool is the country's oldest street tramway. With 11½ miles of standard gauge route along the coast from Starr Gate to Fleetwood it is a delightful ride on a sunny summer's day. This tramway is the most historic of all the mainland tramways. The operating company has recognised this and ensures that guest historic tramcars are used during the season, although many of the trams in the normal operating fleet are historic vehicles in their own right. Some of the trams are painted in historic liveries. The tramway also has the only trailer operation on the mainland. Most of the route is reserved track, though there is an attractive street-running section in Fleetwood and the Fleetwood terminus is by the road-side. Recently a weight limit on the street track meant that double deck tramcars could not run to Fleetwood. This has now been rectified and a full service is operating.

Tickets

Single journey tickets and one day travel cards are available from conductors (or drivers on One Person Operated Cars) on the tramcars. Longer period travelcards cannot be purchased on the tramcars. They are available from Blackpool Bus Station, Tourist Information Centres or selected hotels and newsagents (look for the travel card sign).

Fleet

OMO car, bogie, single deck, totally enclosed, built 1934, rebuilt 1973. In store, no public access

8

Open Boat Class, single deck, open, built 1934

600	602	604	605	607

Replica Vanguard, bogie, single deck, vestibuled, built 1934 rebuilt as Vanguard 1987

619

Brush Railcoach, bogie, single deck, totally enclosed, built 1937

621	623	626	630	632	636	637
622	625	627	631	634	637	

Centenary Class, bogie, single deck, totally enclosed, built 1984-1986

641	643	644	645	646	647	648
642						

Coronation Class, bogie, single deck, totally enclosed, built 1953

660

Twin Cars, (Motor car rebuilt Railcoach), bogie, single deck, totally enclosed, built 1936 rebuilt 1958-1960

671/681   672/682   673/683   674/684   675/685   676/686   677/687

Railcoach Class, Rebuilt 1960, bogie, single deck, totally enclosed, built 1936 rebuilt 1958-1960

678   679   680

Balloon Class, bogie, double deck, totally enclosed, built 1934-1935

700+	704	709	713	717	720	723
701	706#	710	715	718	721	724
702	707*	711	716	719	722	726
703	708	712				

+ *Double Destination boxes; # Open Top, "Princess Alice"; * Rebuilt 1998*

Illuminated tramcars

633   Trawler "Cevic", built 2001.

736   Frigate, built 1965, rebuilt 2004, "HMS Blackpool"

Jubilee Class bogie, double deck, totally enclosed, built 1935 rebuilt 1979 & 1982.

761   762

Historic Tramcars

5   Stockport, 4 wheel, open top, unvestibuled, built 1901.

40   Fleetwood Box, bogie, single deck, totally enclosed, built 1914.

66   Bolton, bogie, enclosed top, unvestibuled, built 1901.

147   Blackpool Standard, built 1924.

304   Blackpool Coronation with Vambac equipment, built 1953.

Works Cars

259   Permanent Way car, bogie, single deck, totally enclosed, built 1937, in store no public access.

260   Rail-crane, Bogie flat floor trailer, built 1973.

750   Reel Wagon, 4 wheel trailer, built 1928.

752   Railgrinder, 4 wheel, Works van, built 1928.

754   Overhead Line Car, open top, vestibuled, built 1992.

938   Ford transit van.

939   Unimog, road-rail.

940   Unimog, road-rail .

941   Bedford Bruff road-rail Tower wagon.

Nearby

Lancastrian Transport Trust Collection.

BOURNEMOUTH CLIFF RAILWAYS

Address

Seafront Information
Undercliffe Drive
Bournemouth
BH2 5AA

Tel: 01202 451781
Web: www.bournemouth.gov.uk
GR: East Cliff   SZ097908
            Fisherman's Walk   SZ110913
            West Cliff   SZ083905
Gauge: East Cliff   5' 6"
            Fisherman's Walk   5' 8"
            West Cliff   5' 6"

Open

All year, though they will be closed some periods during the winter months for maintenance.

How to get there

By public transport: travel by train to Bournemouth station. From here take a bus to the sea front. Along the sea front there are two options, the first is to take one of

The Bournemouth East Cliff funicular.

The funicular at Fisherman's Walk.

the open-top buses that run along the Overcliffe Drive, or along the Undercliffe Drive is a 'Land Train'. Both will connect with the three cliff lifts. The West Cliff Railway is situated close to Bournemouth Pier. From the pier walk west, past the Oceanarium and West Beach Restaurant. The Cliff Railway is a little further on. The East Cliff Railway is about halfway between Bournemouth and Boscombe Piers. Fisherman's Walk Cliff Railway is about the same distance the other side of Boscombe Pier.

By car: from the end (junction 1) of the M27, drive straight onto the A31. Just past Ringwood take the A338 to Bournemouth. Follow the A338, then follow signs

The West Cliff funicular at Bournemouth.

west to Durley Chine where there is on-street parking on West Overcliffe Drive. From the pier walk as above, from Durley Chine proceed along the West Promenade towards the pier. The West Cliff Railway is about 200 yards on the left. The other two railways are too far away by foot. So return to the car and drive past the pier, straight across the roundabout, then first right which takes you to East Overcliffe Drive. The East Cliff Railway is about halfway between Bournemouth and Boscombe Piers. The signs to the Railway are not large. Further along, after weaving around at Boscombe, enter Boscombe Overcliffe Drive until the café at Fisherman's Walk is seen. The Cliff Railway is just past the café, hidden below the top of the cliff.

Description

All three cliff railways are electrically driven and have two cars running on separate 5' 6" gauge tracks, which are far enough apart not to need widening at the passing point. The East Cliff Railway (170ft long) and the West Cliff Railway (145ft long) were both opened in 1908. The Fisherman's Walk Cliff Railway (128ft long) is a relative newcomer, being built in 1935. They are open all year apart from closing for maintenance during the winter months. Check first if visiting during the winter.

The Bridgnorth funicular was constructed in a cutting and is not easily seen.

Tickets

Only single journey tickets are sold and are available from either the upper or lower stations. There may also be a "Freedom" Ticket giving unlimited use of the funiculars and the 'Land Train'.

Nearby

Museum of Electricity, Christchurch, 5 miles to the east.

BRIDGNORTH CLIFF RAILWAY

Address

Bridgnorth Cliff Railway
6A Castle Terrace
Bridgnorth
Shropshire

Tel: 01746 762052 (station), 01746 762124 (Office)
GR: SO720932
Gauge: 3' 8"

Open

All year.

How to get there

By public transport: travel by rail to Kidderminster station, change to the Severn Valley Railway station alongside. Take the SVR to Bridgnorth. From the station exit walk straight ahead and cross the high footbridge. At the far side of the footbridge cross the road and take the steps up to Castle Walk. Turn right along the Walk, with magnificent views across the River Severn. Continue on Castle Walk until you reach the cliff lift.

By car: from junction 4 of the M54 head south following signs for the A442. On reaching the A442 turn south following signs to Bridgnorth or Kidderminster. Keep an eye open because the A442 leaves the big dual carriageway, so make sure you take the correct slip road. If you find that the dual carriageway suddenly becomes a single road, you have missed the turning, so keep on to the next roundabout (with a replica pit head in the centre), go right round, back the way you came, then leave by the first slip road. Follow the A442 to Bridgnorth. Where the built-up part of Bridgnorth starts there is a roundabout, go straight across and then take the first right. This takes you across the bridge (the cliff railway is directly in front of you), follow the signs to the town centre, where there is limited on-street parking. Walk to the end of the High Street and by the Town Hall turn left. Walk past shops to a passageway on the right. Go along the passageway (with more shops) and the cliff railway is about 200 yards on the left.

Description

At one time the cliff railway claimed to be the only inland funicular in the country (which conveniently forgot about Shipley Glen), but with the new funiculars at Cairngorm, Llechwedd, Machynlleth and Windsor the claim is now that Bridgnorth has the oldest and steepest inland funicular. Opened in 1892 on a track gauge of 3' 8" and 201ft long, the railway links the upper and lower halves of the town of Bridgnorth, and is more of a real method of transport than a tourist attraction. Originally operated by water counterbalance the lift was converted to electrical operation in 1943. The two cars run on separate tracks, which are far enough apart not to require widening where the cars cross. The lower part of the journey is in a deep cutting, but the cars emerge into the open in the upper part, giving wonderful views of the Severn Valley. At the top a stroll along Castle Walk is recommended and more vintage transport can be seen on the Severn Valley Railway line.

Tickets

Only return tickets are sold, but are available from either the upper or lower stations.

Nearby

Telford Steam Railway, Horsehay.

CAIRNGORM FUNICULAR RAILWAY, AVIEMORE

Address

Cairngorm Mountain Limited
Aviemore
Inverness-shire
PH22 1RB
Tel: 01479 861261
GR: NH995045
Gauge: 2 metres

Open

All year.

How to get there

Public transport: Travel by rail to Aviemore Station. There is a regular bus service

Opened in 2003 the Cairngorm is Scotland's only funicular and was built to serve the skiers at Aviemore. Photograph David Cole.

from the station to the funicular, which is in Glenmore Forest Park at the end of a mountain road and some five miles from Aviemore station. For the bus timetable phone 01479 811566.

By car: From the end of the M90 head north on the A9. Drive for 60 miles to Aviemore. Take a right turn to Glenmore Forest Park and continue up to the end of the road, where the funicular starts.

Description

Opened in December 2001 the Cairngorm railway is the only funicular in Scotland. It is also unusual in being built on a concrete viaduct, to keep the tracks above the snow in winter, with a final tunnel leading to the upper stations. The two carriages can each seat 48 or 120 standing during the skiing season. It was built principally for the winter months to take skiers up the slopes of the Cairngorms. It is hoped that it will also encourage summer visitors by making the mountain more accessible to visitors. Though, as a landscape conservation measure, summer visitors will not be allowed out of the Visitors Centre. For this purpose there are two upper stations, one used in the winter and one in the summer. So if you want to get on to the mountain in the summer you will have to do it the hard way and walk up. Nearly a mile and a quarter long, it ends 400 feet below the summit at a restaurant and visitor's centre. The journey takes around seven minutes.

Tickets

Only day tickets are sold and are expensive if all you want is a ride on the funicular, the prices being set for skiers who use the funicular several times in the day.

Nearby

Alford Valley Railway and the Grampian Transport Museum are around 50 miles away to the east.

CROYDON TRAMLINK

Address

> Tramlink Croydon Ltd
> Tramlink Information Centre
> Unit 5
> Suffolk House
> George Street
> Croydon

Tel: 020 8681 8300
GR: TQ328654
Gauge: 4' 8½"

Open

All year.

How to get there

By public transport: Tramlink has three routes stretching from Wimbledon in the west to Beckenham and New Addington in the east. Access onto the tramway is probably best by public transport. There is an underground connection (District Line) at Wimbledon and National Railway connections at Wimbledon, Mitcham Junction, East Croydon, West

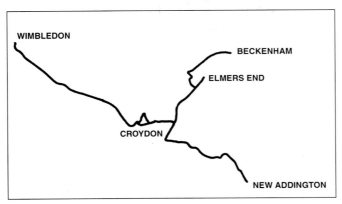

Croydon, Birkbeck, Beckenham and Elmers End. The choice is yours.

By car: From the northern end of the M23 join the A23 heading north. After four miles Purley is reached. Take the A212 to Croydon, three miles from Purley. There is multi-storey parking around the centre, particularly at the Whitgift Shopping Centre. Or drive out on any of the tram routes to find on-street parking away from the centre. But it is not recommended owing to the heavy traffic all around the area.

Description

One of the new generation of tramways in Britain using tramcars built by Bombardier in Vienna of a design very similar to the low floor trams used in Cologne, Germany. The system is a combination of road and reserved track, with the latter having the most route miles, the road sections being in the busy shop-

The Croydon Tramlink has a single track that loops around the centre of Croydon.

ping centres of Croydon. To accommodate the tramway a Central Croydon Loop of single track has been built around the town centre. This provides some superb views as the tramcars run by shops that also saw the trams of London Transport pre-1952. As the new trams are also painted red and white the scene is very nostalgic. The run along George Street, down Church Street and at Reeves Corner is particularly recommended. There is also a quite rural section across Shirley Park and Addington Hills and down Gravel Hill to Addington Village. The more urban sections include the reserved track run to Wimbledon and out to Beckenham Junction and a short spur to Elmers End. The depot is by Therapia Lane stop. The unusual fleet numbering is related to the historical London Transport Tramways system. The highest number tramcar was 2529, the Croydon Tramlink continues this numbering by starting at 2530.

Tickets
Tickets are available from ticket machines at the stops. However, most people will be travelling to Croydon by public transport using travel cards (sold at all tube stations). The appropriate Zone(s) travel card is valid on the tram and allows unlimited travel. Travel cards are not sold by the machines, but are available at East Croydon and West Croydon stations.

Fleet
6 axle, single deck articulated, totally enclosed, built 1998-1999

2530	2534	2538	2542	2545	2548	2551
2531	2535	2539	2543	2546	2549	2552
2532	2536	2540	2544	2547	2550	2553
2533	2537	2541				

Nearby
Docklands Light Railway, London Transport Museum, Covent Garden, London funicular.

DOCKLANDS LIGHT RAILWAY, LONDON

Address
Docklands Light Railway Limited
Docklands Railway Management Ltd
Castor Lane
London
E14 0DS

Tel: 020 7363 9500.

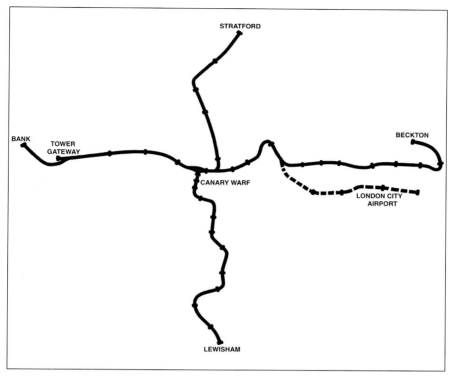

Travel Hotline: 020 7918 4000
GR: TQ379806
Gauge: 4' 8½"

Open
All year.

How to get there
By public transport: Like all transport in London I would recommend parking on the outskirts of London and going in by public transport. An All Zones day ticket gives freedom of travel around the whole network. Access to the Docklands tramway via the tube is available at Bank, Tower Gateway, Bow Church or Stratford stations. There are connections with the national railway network at Stratford, Limehouse, Custom House, Canning Town, Greenwich and Lewisham.
By car: It really is not worth it, particularly with the London Congestion Charges. Like all transport in London I would recommend parking on the outskirts of London and going in by public transport.

Tickets

Tickets are available from ticket machines at the stops. However, most people will be travelling to Docklands by public transport using travel cards (sold at all tube stations). The appropriate Zone(s) travel card is valid on the light railway and allows unlimited travel.

Description

The London Docklands Light Railway is a wholly reserved track system operating with a third rail using 750 volts DC. The system has been extended since first opening and now has around 18 miles of route, running from the city (Bank Station) to Stratford, or Beckton, or Lewisham. The busiest part of the system is the junction between the route and this is best seen from West India Quay station. The most impressive station is just one stop away at Canary Warf. The main depot (no public access) is at Poplar and a second one (no public access) is between Galleons Reach and Beckton. The building of a new branch has been started from Canning Town to link with London City Airport and which may also be extended under the River Thames to Woolwich Arsenal. Due to open in 2005 the new branch will have stations at West Silvertown, Pontoon Dock, London City Airport and King George V.

Fleet

B90 Class, 6 axle, single deck articulated, totally enclosed, built 1991

22	26	30	33	36	39	42
23	27	31	34	37	40	43
24	28	32	35*	38	41	44
25	29					

* *Converted to B92 standard before delivery.*

B92 Class, 6 axle, single deck articulated, totally enclosed, built 1992

45	52	59	66	73	80	86
46	53	60	67	74	81	87
47	54	61	68	75	82	88
48	55	62	69	76	83	89
49	56	63	70	77	84	90
50	57	64	71	78	85	91
51	58	65	72	79		

B92 Class, 6 axle, single deck articulated, totally enclosed, built 2002.

92	96	01	05	08	11	14
93	97	02	06	09	12	15
94	98	03	07	10	13	16
95	99	04				

The Docklands Light Railway has been a great success, with an extension recently opened to Lewisham and another soon to open to London City Airport.

Works Cars

Wickham model CT30 0-4-0 motor trolley, with hydraulic crane, supplied 1986
    92

Battery electric locomotive 0-4-0, RFS with hydraulic crane, built 1991
    93

Diesel locomotive 0-4-0, GEC with Gardner engine, built 1979
    94

Diesel locomotive 0-4-0, Ruston, built 1962
    95

Rail crane bogie flat wagon
    96

Bogie flat wagon, two half freightliner unit ends joined back to back
    97

Bogie wagon three plank, two half freightliner unit ends joined back to back
    98

Bogie flat wagon, two half freightliner unit ends joined back to back
    99

Ballast hopper bogie wagon, made by Plasser from a ballast cleaning machine
    100

Nearby
Croydon Tramlink, London Transport Museum, Covent Garden and London funicular.

DOUGLAS ISLE OF MAN HORSE TRAMWAY

Address
>Douglas Corporation
>Strathallan Crescent
>Douglas, Isle of Man
>IM2 4NR

Tel: 01624 696420
GR: SC394775
Gauge: 3' 0"

Open
1 May to 28 September.

How to get there
By public transport: There are two ways to get to the Isle of Man. By air to Ronaldsway Airport or by ferry landing at Douglas. By the latter the horse tramway is just a short walk from the harbour.

By car: The ferry takes road vehicles and will land you in Douglas. The horse tramway starts a short distance from the harbour. Parking in Douglas centre is disc controlled. Discs are free and can be obtained at the Tourist Information Centre at the harbour. But parking time is strictly limited. The best option is to drive along the promenade until you leave the disc zone, about half way along. There are no parking restrictions from this point onward.

Description
Probably the last public horse tramway

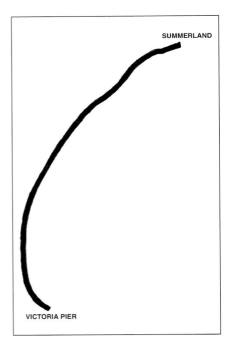

SUMMERLAND

VICTORIA PIER

The Douglas Horse Tramway is possibly the last public horse tramway in the world.

in the world outside a museum or theme park. The 3' 0" gauge system runs about 1½ miles along the sweep of Douglas Bay from Douglas harbour to meet the Manx Electric line at Derby Castle. The history of the tramway reaches back to the earliest days of tramways in Britain. First proposed in 1875 it opened in 1876 and apart from doubling the original single track the system is very much the same as it was in the old days. Taking a ride on the tramway is stepping back over a hundred years. The depot is at Derby Castle terminus and it is usually open to allow visitors see more historic horse trams, a display of items regarding the Douglas cable tramway and the restored cable tramcar number 72/73. The stables are near the Derby Castle terminus and it is common to see the changing of horses, as each horse is only allowed to do a few trips each day. Less common is the sight of horses training on the beach. New horses are trained by dragging a wooden sledge along the beach, getting them used to the pull of the tram and the frequent stops.

Tickets

Three-day "Freedom" tickets cover all public road transport on the island, including the horse trams. These can be purchased from all main train stations, tram stations at Douglas, Laxey and Ramsey, IoM Transport booking office or the Tourist Information Centre, Douglas Sea Terminal; selected hotels and shops also sell them. Otherwise it is necessary to purchase a return ticket only valid on day of issue (no single tickets are issued).

Fleet
4 wheel, single deck, saloon, built 1913
  1
4 wheel, single deck, toastrack, built 1886
  11
4 wheel, single deck, toastrack, built 1888
  12
4 wheel, double deck, open top, built 1883
  18
4 wheel, single deck, toastrack, built 1890
  21   22 Converted to Saloon, tram shop selling souvenirs
4 wheel, single deck, saloon, built 1892
  27   28   29
4 wheel, single deck, toastrack, built 1896
  32   33   34   35   36   37
4 wheel, single deck, toastrack, built 1902
  38   39   40 in store
4 wheel, Single Deck, toastrack, built 1905-1911
  42   43   44   45
Upper Douglas Cable Tramway, bogie, single deck, crossbench, built 1896. A single tramcar constructed from the remaining parts of two.
  72/73

Nearby
At the Derby Castle terminus is the Manx Electric Railway, at Laxey is the Snaefell Mountain Railway. Also in Douglas is the Manx Museum, while across the island in Peel is the Manx Transport Museum.

DUBLIN LUAS

Address

Railway Procurement Agency
Parkgate Business Centre
Parkgate Street
Dublin 8
Ireland
Tel: +353 (01) 646 3400
Web: www.luas.ie
Gauge: 4' 8½"

At last a new Luas tramcar in service. Photograph Adam Winstanley.

Open
All year.

How to get there
By public transport: Travel by rail to Connelly Station where there is an interchange with Luas.

By car: Drive into Dublin and park in one of the city centre car parks. Make your way to Connelly station to pick up the tramway on the Red Line or the Green Line.

Description
Not to be confused with DART (Dublin Area Rapid Transit) which is a suburban railway

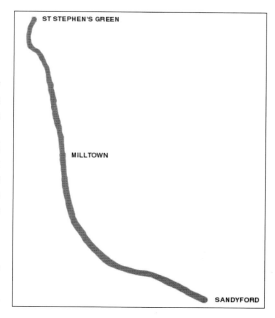

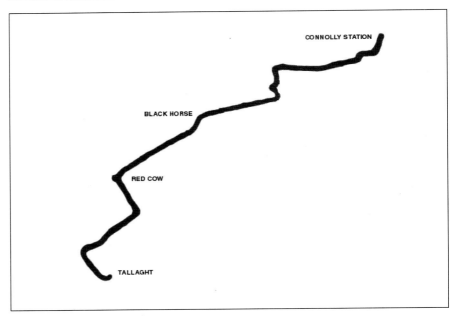

system, the LUAS is the first of the new generation of tramways to be built in Ireland. The system has two routes, the first is called the Green Line, while the second is the Red Line. The Red Line is not connected to the Green Line. The Green Line runs from Connelly Station to Tallaght and has the type 301 cars, while the Red Line runs from St Stephen's Green to Sandyford and has the 401 cars. The Green line opened on 30th June 2004 and the Red line on 28th September 2004. For information contact the Railway Procurement Agency. The operator is Connex, but no details of contact points have been announced.

Tickets
There are no conductors on the trams. Tickets must be purchased prior to boarding from machines at each stop.

Fleet
Type 301, 6 axle, Alstom Citidis single deck articulated tramcars, totally enclosed, built 2003.
26 cars

3001	3005	3009	3013	3017	3021	3024
3002	3006	3010	3014	3018	3022	3025
3003	3007	3011	3015	3019	3023	3026
3004	3008	3012	3016	3020		

Type 401, 8 axle, Alstom Citidis single deck articulated tramcars, totally enclosed, built 2003.
14 cars

4001	4003	4005	4007	4009	4011	4013
4002	4004	4006	4008	4010	4012	4014

Nearby
National Transport Museum, Howth Castle, Fry model railway Malahide Castle

FOLKESTONE CLIFF RAILWAY

Address
        Shepway District Council
        Civic Centre
        Castle Hill Avenue
        Folkestone
        CT20 2QY
Tel: 01303 251573
Web: www.shepway.gov.uk
GR: TR225358
Gauge: 5' 10"

One of the few funiculars still operating on the water balance principle. The track on the right is the 1890 funicular that was closed in 1967.

Open
Easter to October inclusive

How to get there
By public transport: travel by rail to Folkestone Central station. Leave station and walk along Cheriton Road into town. At the junction with Cheriton Gardens bear right into Cheriton Gardens, then Cheriton Place. At the end turn left into Sandgate Road towards McDonalds and Pelosi's Coffee Bar. Then take the right turn into West Terrace leading to the War Memorial. Turn right into The Leas, and about 100 yards on the left is the upper station of the Cliff Railway.
By car: from the end (junction 13) of the M20 head for the Hoverspeed Seacat Terminal. When at the end of Harbour Approach, by the Rotunda Fun Park, turn right into Marine Parade. Follow this, which becomes Lower Sandgate Road. The lower station of the cliff railway is along this road on the right. There is plenty of parking near to the cliff railway.

Description
At one time Folkestone had four cliff railways, unfortunately three have closed, including one that ran immediately alongside the remaining operating railway. The Leas Cliff Railway was opened in 1885 with 164ft of 5' 10" gauge track. This is one of the true water displacement types of cliff railways. Originally the used water in the lower car was allowed to drain to the beach. From 1890 pumps were fitted to recycle the water. The railway operates by the brakesman releasing the brakes and opening the valve to allow water to enter the tank of the top car. When the weight is greater than the lower car they both move and the water valve is closed. On some occasions the number of passengers in the upper car will be enough to raise an empty lower car and no water is needed. Watching the process from the top is recommended. The descending car does not switch off the water until it has moved a short distance, by which time the side of the car is given a wash. The abandoned second Leas Cliff Railway (4' 10" gauge) alongside was constructed in 1890 and closed in 1967. When in the lower station building, take a few minutes to examine the unusual model of the system in the cabinet fixed to the wall. A carriage from the second line alongside the Leas Cliff Railway is preserved at Dover Transport Museum.

Tickets
Single tickets only, which are sold at the lower station. Passengers travelling down pay on arrival at the lower station.

Nearby
Folkestone is somewhat isolated from other tramway interest. There is a Transport

Museum at Dover, some 9 miles along the coast, but the only tram (a Maidstone demi-car) is not on public display yet. The nearest other points of interest are the two funiculars at Hastings about 40 miles to the west.

GATWICK AIRPORT PEOPLE MOVER

Address

British Airports Authority
Gatwick Airport
Surrey
Tel: 0870 000 2468
GR: TQ280410
Gauge: Rubber tyres on concrete track

Open
All year.

How to get there
By public transport: Travel by rail to Gatwick Station. The station is at the South Terminal building. Follow the signs to airport arrivals and departures. Just before the main hall there is a sign pointing right to North Terminal, so turn right into corridor and follow to the end where the people mover is.

At Gatwick Airport a cable operated tramway connects the two terminal buildings.

By car: From junction 9 of the M23 follow the signs for Gatwick Airport, turning right on to a motorway spur leading to the end (junction 9A). From here follow the signs to the South Terminal buildings. Approaching the buildings follow the signs for short term parking and park in any one of the multi-storey car parks (very expensive). On foot follow the signs for arrivals and departures. In the departures hall look for the signs to the North Terminal, or the railway station. On leaving the hall into the corridor leading to the railway station almost immediately turn left into a corridor marked North Terminal. The people mover is at the end of the corridor.

Description

Gatwick Airport has two large terminal buildings that are some distance apart. To facilitate passenger movement between the terminals there is a people mover. It consists of a fully automated double track line between the two terminals. In reality the tracks are operated as two independent single track lines. For most of the time only one track is operated, giving a six-minute service. At peak periods the second track is also used to give a three-minute service. Each track has a three-carriage unit, electrically powered with rubber tyres and guided by a central rail which incorporates the power supply. It is open to anyone and there is no charge for using it.

Tickets

Free, no tickets required.

Fleet

Two three-car units, one on each track. No fleet numbers visible.

Nearby

The Volks Railway is about 30 miles south in Brighton.

GLASGOW UNDERGROUND

Address

Glasgow Underground Railway
Strathclyde Passenger Transport
Broomloan Depot
Robert Street
Govan
Glasgow
G51 2BY

Cowcaddens station on the Glasgow underground. Note flash photography is prohibited on all underground railways for safety reasons.

Tel: Traveline 0870 6082608
Web: www.spt.co.uk
Travel Line: 0141 226 4826
GR: NS539658
Gauge: 4' 0"

Open
All year.

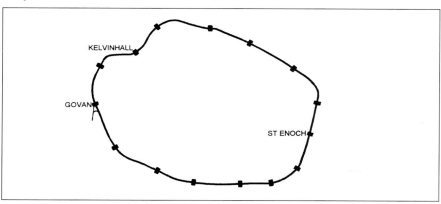

How to get there

By public transport: travel by rail to Glasgow Central station. St. Enoch Underground station is close to the railway station. Walk east down Argyle Street about 100 yards, St. Enoch station is on the right.

By car: Glasgow city centre is not recommended as parking is difficult. There are car parks at Shields Road, West Street and Bridge Street stations south of the Clyde and Kelvinbridge station north of the river. All car parks are equipped with closed circuit TV surveillance, and inclusive tickets for car parking and return journey are available.

Description

For a city that has been the European City of Culture and has produced the Rangers and Celtic football teams, Glasgow is amazingly reticent about its Underground. During my recent visit I was accompanied by a fellow enthusiast from Austria. We walked towards an Underground station and one shop away I asked him if he could see the station. His reply, as I expected, was no. So we walked to the entrance and I asked again if he could see the Underground station. Again the response was no. He was astonished when I turned the corner and took him down some steps to the ticket office. This reluctance by Glasgow to admit to visitors that it has an underground has always surprised me. There is every reason to broadcast to the nation that the Underground is a quick, inexpensive and enjoyable way around the city. Originally cable hauled and then electrified in 1934, the whole system was rebuilt between 1977 and 1980. New rolling stock replaced the original 1896 trains and a ramp was built to connect the running lines to the depot, closing the old carriage lift. The link is visible between Govan and Ibrox stations. When the Glaswegians saw the vivid orange colour of the new carriages the system was immediately called after a contemporary film, "Clockwork Orange". A circle of 15 stations gives two travelling options, clockwise, or anticlockwise!

Tickets

Tickets are sold at every Underground station. The Discovery ticket, valid after 9.30 Mon-Sat and all day Sunday, gives a day's unlimited travel for less than the normal return fare.

Fleet

Bogie single deck power cars, built 1977-79

101	106	111	116	121	126	130
102	107	112	117	122	127	131
103	108	113	118	123	128	132
104	109	114	119	124	129	133
105	110	115	120	125		

Bogie single deck trailers, built 1992

201	203	204	205	206	207	208
202						

4 wheel battery electric locomotives, built 1977 and 1974

L2 Lobey Dosser
L3 Rank Bajin
L4 El Fideldo

Nearby
Glasgow Museum of Transport and Coatbridge Summerlee Heritage Park.

GREAT ORME CABLE TRAMWAY

Address

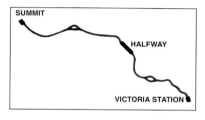

Great Orme Tramway
Victoria Station, Church Walks
Llandudno
Tel: 01492 574237
Web: www.greatormetramway.com
GR: SH779824
Gauge: 3' 6"

Open
Easter to First Week in October.

How to get there
By public transport: travel by rail to Llandudno station. Follow the main shopping street (Mostyn Street) up to the Empire Hotel, turn left into Church Walks, and the tramway terminus is on the right.

By car: Llandudno is just off the A55 in North Wales. The most appropriate route is to turn off the A55 at Llandrillo yn Rhos onto the B5115, and then to head for Rhos-on-Sea and the approach to Llandudno which follows the route of the former Llandudno and Colwyn Bay Electric Railway. Once on the main shopping street in Llandudno (Mostyn Street) drive up to the Empire Hotel, turn left into Church Walks and Victoria Station, the end of the tramway, is on the right. On-street car parking is available, but well used in the season.

Description
Strictly speaking this is not a cable tramway but two separate funiculars because the trams are fixed to the cables. The winding motors for the 3' 6" gauge tramway

A new station, winding house and museum has been opened at Halfway on the Great Orme Tramway.

are situated at the Halfway Station and power both halves of the line. Passengers have to change trams at the halfway point. The first part of the journey is over a road section, then the remainder is on reserved track. The original overhead wires (used for communications) were removed as contact between the tramcars and the winding motor operator is now by radio. However, the overhead has recently been reinstalled as part of the renovation programme. Superb photos can be taken on the lower section where the tramcars can be seen with a backdrop of the whole of Llandudno and the Little Orme.

Tickets
Tickets are sold at the ticket office at Victoria Station, the lower end of the tramway.

Fleet
Bogie, single deck saloon, unvestibuled, built 1902 & 1903.
   4 "St Tudno"   5 "St Silio"   6 "St Seiriol"   7 "St Trillo"

Nearby
Mostyns Cafe (in the Model Tramway section of the book).

HASTINGS CLIFF RAILWAYS

Address

Hastings Tourist Information Centre
Queens Square
Priory Meadow
Hastings

Tel: 01424 781111
Web: www.hastings.gov.uk
GR: East Cliff   TQ827095
           West Cliff   TQ822094
Gauge: East Cliff 5' 0"
           West Cliff 6' 0"

Open

All year

How to get there

By public transport: travel by rail to Hastings station. Leave station and walk along Havelock Road towards the sea front. At the end turn left into East Parade and walk towards the harbour. Bear left into George Street, and the West Cliff Railway lower station is along the street on the left. After visiting the West Cliff Railway, walk out of the lower station, and keep straight down the passage to East Parade. Turn left and you will see the East Lift about 500 yards away in Rock-a-Nore Road.

By car: there is no close motorway. Enter Hastings either by the A21 (drive down to the front and turn left into the A259) or the A259. The West Cliff Railway is easily seen from the A259 when travelling east. If travelling west, the railway is hidden until it is behind you. Drive to the harbour area by the Fisherman's Museum in Rock-a-Nore Street. There is a large pay and display car park which is convenient for the East Cliff Railway. The West Cliff Railway is a comfortable walk away.

Description

The two Hastings cliff railways each have their own attractions for the funicular enthusiast. The West Cliff Railway has the very unusual feature of travelling in a tunnel for most of its length. Of the 500ft of travel, some 363ft are inside the tunnel. Construction of the railway was assisted by natural caverns and much of the brick-lined tunnel was constructed inside such a cavern. The track gauge is 6' (rail centre to rail centre), and each car runs on its own tracks which are sufficiently apart not to need widening at the passing point. The upper station is close to the Castle and St. Clement's caves. Originally powered by gas and diesel engines, the

The Hastings East Hill funicular gives wonderful views over the town.

The West Hill funicular at Hastings is almost entirely in a tunnel, unusual in Britain.

railway was converted to electric motor power in 1971.

The East Cliff Railway is called "Ooh what a whopper" by its owners the Hastings Council, though with a track length of 265ft it is considerably shorter than the West Cliff Railway. However, the siting of the railway is spectacular and views from it are superb. It leads to the start of Hastings Country Park, a 600 acre area of unspoilt countryside open to the public and well worth a visit. The railway opened in 1902 and was originally worked by water counterbalance. In 1976, after a three year closure, the railway reopened powered by an electric motor.

Tickets
Return tickets only, sold at the lower station.

HYTHE PIER TRAMWAY

Address

Hythe Pier
Hythe
Hampshire
Tel: 023 8084 0722
GR: SU424084
Gauge: 2' 0"

Open
All year except Christmas and Boxing Days.

How to get there
By public transport: The easiest and most interesting way of getting to the pier is to go to Southampton by bus or train and take the ferry across to Hythe, the pier and the tramway. By rail go to Southampton Central, walk to Town Quay (about a mile). Make sure you do not take the Isle of Wight Ferry by mistake.

By car: From Junction 2 of the M27 take the A326 south for about 8 miles. Follow signs to the left to Hythe (road has no number). The pier is at the northern end of the main shopping street. Hythe has ample car parking for the shopping centre. Or go by water using the ferry from Southampton.

Description
Hythe Pier was built in 1881 with a 2' 0" gauge hand-operated tramway being installed in 1909. In 1922 the tramway was electrified with a third rail to carry passengers to and from the ferry boats. Today the ferry boat "Hotspur" provides a link between Hythe and Southampton, Town Key. The electric tram is a free

One of the Hythe Pier locomotives, both are to the same unusual design. The tramway was re-opened after damage to the pier in 2003.

service for ferry passengers, who get priority on the trams. Non-ferry visitors can visit the pier for a small toll and ride the tram for a further fare. The pier is just under half a mile long and the electric tramway runs the full length. Power is 240 volts through a third rail supply. Photography on the pier itself is somewhat restricted due to its narrow width. To get a good picture of the whole tram train, walk along the shopping street for a couple of hundred yards. Then there is access to the riverside and by walking back to the pier the whole side of the pier is on view. Make sure you get a ride on the tramway as its unsprung carriages are a unique travelling experience. On 1 November 2003 the pier was damaged by a dredger colliding with it, creating an eighteen feet gap in the structure. Thankfully the pier tramway was reopened for passengers on 6 January 2004.

Tickets
The tramway is free to passengers on the ferry. Otherwise tickets are sold at the pier entrance. Note: if the tram is full, preference is given to ferry passengers.

Fleet
4 wheel, steeple cab electric locomotives, built 1917
    1   2
Two, bogie, single deck, totally enclosed, driver trailers, built 1921, no numbers.
Two, bogie, single deck, totally enclosed, trailers, built 1921, no numbers.

The funicular by the Millennium Bridge is for disabled passengers only.

One, 4 wheel, flat bed luggage trolley, built 1909, no number.
One, 4 wheel, tank truck, no number

Nearby
The nearest other attractions are the three funiculars at Bournemouth and the model tramway at Wimborne, both to the west of Hythe.

LONDON FUNICULAR, MILLENNIUM BRIDGE

Address Not known
GR: TQ325810
Gauge: 1m

Open
All year except Christmas and Boxing Days.

How to get there
Public transport: As with all London attractions public transport is by far the best way. Go to Blackfriars station on the Circle/District line. From the station take the Queen Victoria Street south exit. Turn right and walk eastwards parallel with the river. Do not be tempted to take any of the roads down to the river – the road system is such that pedestrians going that way end up in the middle of a fast dual carriageway with no escape. Keep walking along Queen Victoria Street until you reach Peters Hill. This is unmistakable as to the left is a fine view of St Paul's and to the right is the Millennium foot bridge, leading to the Tate Modern. So turn right and walk towards the bridge. Just before the bridge take the steps on the right leading down to the embankment. The funicular is beside these steps.
By car: It is not worth thinking about.

Description
I was rather puzzled by this funicular as there was no indication of how to use it and it was not working at all on the two occasions that I visited it. Later I discovered why. It was still in the process of being finished. It actually did not open until 5 December 2003. Built by Maspero Elevatori of Italy, it is a sloping lift for disabled people. The official title is an "Inclinator", presumably a cross between an elevator and an incline. I much prefer funicular. It is very much hidden away. The best way if finding it is to walk on the north embankment under the footbridge, it is on the east side of the bridge built alongside an office block. It has a single carriage running on rails at the same slope as the stairs next to it (13.6 degrees). It is panelled in with glass sheets, so is very visible.

Tickets
There is no charge for disabled passengers.

Nearby
Croydon Tramlink, Docklands Light Railway and London Transport Museum, Covent Garden.

LYNTON AND LYNMOUTH CLIFF RAILWAY

Address
Lynton & Lynmouth Lift Company
Lynmouth
Devon

Tel: 01598 753486
Web: www.cliffrailwaylynton.co.uk
GR: SS718497
Gauge: 3' 9"

Open
February to November inclusive

How to get there
By public transport: it is not easy or quick to get to Lynton or Lynmouth by public transport. Travel by rail to Taunton station. Catch a bus via Minehead. Alternatively from Taunton get a 28A (weekdays or 928 Sundays) bus to Bishop's Lydeard and take the West Somerset Railway to Minehead. Then take a bus to Lynton. The Cliff Railway is well signposted.
By car: from junction 23 of the M5 head towards Bridgewater on the A38. Look for the signs to Minehead (A39) and follow them to Minehead. At Minehead follow the signs to Lynmouth going over the exciting Porlock Hill. At Lynmouth my advice is to continue up the hill to Lynton where there are car parks and limited on-street parking. The upper station of the cliff railway is well signposted, and is a couple of minutes walk from the Town Hall.

Description
Lynton and Lynmouth is one of the more famous of Britain's cliff railways. Initiated by George Newnes, the publisher, the railway opened in 1890 and at 862ft long it is the longest in the country and has the highest rise, some 500ft. The twin tracks are 3' 9" gauge and set closely together so that they diverge at the passing place to allow the two cars to pass without contact. The power is the traditional

Britain's most famous funicular connects Lynton with Lynmouth.

water counterbalance, the used water in the lower car being allowed to run to the sea at the end of each journey. While on the railway, look out for the upper of the three footbridges across the track. On the higher side of the bridge can be seen the remains of platforms either side of the track. This was an intermediate stopping place which was closed in 1932 to speed up the service.

Tickets
Single and return tickets are available from ticket offices at the upper and lower stations.

Nearby
The Lynton Cliff railway is rather isolated from other attractions, the nearest being Launceston Railway about 50 miles to the west and the Torquay Babbacombe Cliff Railway some 70 miles by road to the south.

MANCHESTER METROLINK

Address
Serco Metrolink Ltd
Metrolink House
Queens Road
Manchester
M8 0RY

Tel: 0161 205 8665. **Passenger Enquiries:** 0161 205 2000
GR: SD849006
Gauge: 4' 8½"

Open
All year.

How to get there
By public transport: there is direct rail interchange at the following railway stations: Manchester Piccadilly, Manchester Victoria, Manchester G-Mex, Stretford and Altrincham.
By car: The Metrolink route runs from Bury in the north to Altrincham in the south and Eccles in the west. It is recommended to park on the outer sections of the route and ride into the city centre by tram.

Description
Manchester Metrolink was the first of the new street running light rail networks

to be built in Britain and as such has carved a place for itself in British tramway history. Though most of the 17 miles of standard gauge route is on reserved track, the city centre section is street running. Most of this is shared only with other public transport vehicles, but there is a short length shared with other road users. The system uses raised platforms (even in the street sections) to enable level access to the trams, helping the disabled and those with push chairs. Good overhead views can be gained from the multistorey car park next to the Arndale shopping centre in the middle of the city. Most of the central area can provide interesting backdrops for the trams.

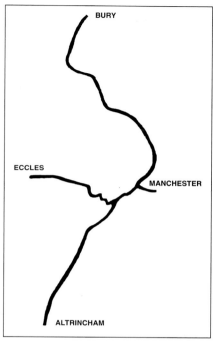

The reserved track sections are less interesting, though the bridge over the River Irwell at Radcliffe on the Bury line is worth a stop. The newest part is the branch from Cornbrook to Eccles where the tramway weaves a tight route around the new office blocks. The depot (no public access) is situated between Victoria and Woodlands Road stops.

Tickets

Tickets are available from machines at all the stops. The off peak day ticket is still available and is marginally easier to buy from the machine than previously.

Fleet

I would like to thank Paul Yearsley for providing the information on the Manchester Fleet.

6 axle, single deck articulated, totally enclosed, built 1991-1992.

1001
1002 "The Mary Sumner"
1003 "The Railway Mission"
1004 "The Robert Owen"
1005
1006
1007 "Sony Centre Arndale"

Manchester Metrolink was the first new generation street running tramway in the country. Its success can be measured by the ever increasing number of routes.

1008 "Erotica G-Mex 2004"
1009
1010 "Golden Jubilee"
1011 "Superb"
1012 "Catherine Hallet"
1013 "Grenadier Guardsman"
1014 "Christies"
1015 "Skill City"
1016 "Erotica G-Mex 2004"
1017 "Bury Hospice"
1018 "Sir Matt Busby"
1019
1020 "David Graham CBE"
1021 "Sony Centre Arndale"
1022 "The Poppy Appeal"
1023
1024 "John Greenwood"
1025
1026 "The Power"

6 axle, single deck articulated, totally enclosed, built 1999-2000
- 2001 "Joe Clark OBE"
- 2002 "Sony Centre Arndale"
- 2003 "Traveller 2000"
- 2004 "Salford Lads Club"
- 2005 "W H Smith West One"
- 2006 "Sony Centre Arndale"

Works Car
One: 4 wheel Open Wagon, built 1991, no number

Metrolink also purchased two San Francisco Boeing tramcars and shipped them over for trials. The expense to bring them up to EEC requirements proved too great, so they never went into service. At the time of writing one is in the Metrolink depot and the other at Serco, Derby.

    1226 (at Derby)   1326 (at Manchester)

Nearby

The Heaton Park Vintage Tramway is a short walk from Heaton Park Metrolink stop and the Manchester Museum of Transport is near Woodlands Road stop (interesting as it has the pre-production mock-up Metrolink tram number 1000).

MANX ELECTRIC RAILWAY

Address

    Isle of Man Transport
    Transport Headquarters
    Banks Circus
    Douglas
    Isle of Man
    IM1 5PY

Tel: 01624 663366.
Fax: 01624663637
Web: wwwgov.iom/tourism
GR: SC394775
Gauge: 3' 0"

Open

Daily Easter to October, summer service May to end August. Monday to Friday November to March.

This is tramcar 2 which, with number 1, are the oldest tramcars in the world that are still used in regular passenger service.

How to get there

By public transport: There are two ways to get to the Isle of Man. By air to Ronaldsway Airport, or by ferry landing at Douglas. By the latter take the horse tramway to Derby Castle where the Manx Electric Tramway starts.

By car: The ferry takes road vehicles and will land you in Douglas. Drive the full length of the promenade to Derby Castle where the Manx Electric Railway starts. Parking is fairly easy.

Description

The Isle of Man has rightly been described as the home of Victorian Transport. The jewel in the crown is the Manx Electric Railway. Over 100 years old it still runs some of the original tramcars in regular service. The eighteen miles of 3' 0" gauge tramway runs along the coast from Douglas Bay to Ramsey. At Laxey it meets the Snaefell Mountain Tramway. There are superb views on the way to Ramsey, where a small Visitor Centre offers an exhibition of the history of the line, tramcar number 59 and a chance to pretend to drive a tramcar. On busy summer days the section between Douglas and Laxey has extra trams in service. The main depot is at Derby Castle (normally no public access) with two other depots at Laxey (no public access) and Ramsey (no public access). Tram driving courses are also offered, pre-booking is necessary. The depot at Laxey was recently closed owing to an unsafe roof and the tramcars it held have been placed in temporary store in the old Homefield Bus Garage in Douglas, where there is no public access. It is very heartening to see that the track is being renewed. The scrapping of works van 14 prompted the Manx Electric Railway Society to contact the Manx Minister for Tourism and Leisure and an undertaking has now been given that no rolling stock or buildings on either the MER or the SMR will be destroyed or dismantled without prior consultation with interested parties and all alternatives being considered. A policy has been agreed that recognises the historic importance of the two lines.

Tickets

Single, return, one day, three day, five day and seven day tickets are sold in the ticket offices at

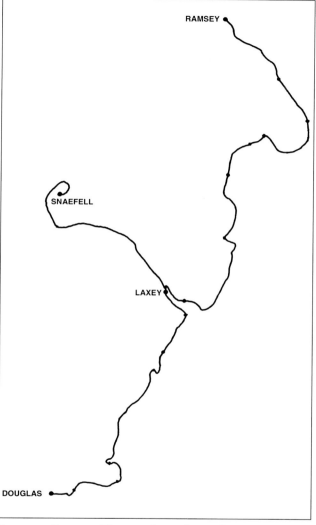

Douglas, Derby Castle, Laxey, or Ramsey. The one, three, five and seven-day "Rail Rover" tickets cover scheduled journeys on the steam railway, electric railway (including the illuminated tram rides), mountain railway, buses and horse trams, but not the Groudle Glen or Orchid lines. All the day or multi-day tickets can be purchased from all main train stations, tram stations at Douglas, Laxey and Ramsey or the Tourist Information Centre, Douglas Sea Terminal; selected hotels and shops also sell them.

Fleet

Bogie, single deck saloon, unvestibuled, built 1893

    1   2

Bogie, single deck, totally enclosed, built 1894

    5   6   7   9*

Illuminated tramcar

Bogie Trailer, single deck, cross bench, unvestibuled, 1893

    13

Bogie, single deck, cross bench, unvestibuled, built 1898

    14*   15*   16   17*   18

* In store, no public access.

Bogie, Winter Saloon, single deck, totally enclosed, built 1899

    19   20   21   22 (Body rebuilt 1992 after a fire)

Bogie, single deck, open wagon goods car, built 1900, rebuilt 1926, owned by Isle of Man Railway and Tramway Preservation Society.

    23 "Dr R Preston Hendry".

Bogie 'Paddleboxes', single deck, cross bench, unvestibuled, built 1893 as trailers rebuilt 1903.

    25   26   27*

* Works Car with temporary vestibules.

Bogie, single deck, cross bench, unvestibuled, built 1904

    28*   29*   30*   31*

* In store, no public access.

Bogie, single deck, cross bench, unvestibuled, built 1906

    32   33

Bogie Trailer, single deck, cross bench, vestibuled built 1894

    36*   37

* In store, no public access.

Bogie Trailer, single deck, cross bench, vestibuled, built 1930

    40   41   44

Bogie Trailer, single deck, cross bench, vestibuled, built 1903

    42   43

Bogie Trailer, single deck, cross bench, vestibuled, built 1899

    45   46   47   48

Bogie Trailer, single deck, cross bench, vestibuled, built 1893

    49   50*   53*   54*

* In store, no public access.

Bogie Trailer, single deck, cross bench, vestibuled, built 1904.

    55   56#   57   58

Rebuilt as totally enclosed trailer for disabled passengers 1995.

Bogie Trailer, single deck, saloon, unvestibuled, built 1904

57   58
Bogie Trailer 'Royal Saloon', single deck, vestibuled, built 1895
    59 On display in Ramsey Visitor Centre.
Bogie Trailer, single deck, cross bench, vestibuled, built 1896
    60
Bogie Trailer, single deck, cross bench, vestibuled, built 1906
    61   62
Bogie, single deck, totally enclosed, built 1906, ex Lisbon Tramways, body used
as waiting room at Derby Castle
    360

Freight and Service Vehicles
4 wheel, 6 ton Open Wagon, built 1894 & 1897
    1   7   8
4 wheel, 6 ton Van, built 1894, 1896 & 1899
    3   4   11   12*
Now Tower Van with ridge roof.
4 wheel, 5 ton Van, built 1903.
    13
4 wheel, Tower Van/Mobile Workshop, built 1908
    16
Bogie, Flat Wagon with Cranes, converted from power car 11 in 1911/26/77
    21
Bogie, Ballast Hopper Trailer, converted from power car 10 in 1918 and rebuilt
2000
    26
Bogie, Flat Wagon, Rail Carrier, converted from trailer 52 in 1947
    52

There is also a demountable Generator Van that was used to power a tram on the
steam railway.

Nearby
At the Derby Castle terminus is the Douglas Horse Tramway. At Laxey is the
connection with the Snaefell Mountain Railway. Also in Douglas is the Manx
Museum, while across the island in Peel is the Manx Transport Museum.

Midland Metro tram 3 at Snow Hill station, Birmingham.

MIDLAND METRO

Address

Travel Midland Metro
Metro Centre
Potters Lane
Wednesbury
West Midlands
WS10 0AR

Tel: 0121 502 2006
GR: SO982946
Gauge: 4' 8"

Open

All year.

How to get there

By public transport: there is direct rail interchange at the following stations:

Birmingham Snow Hill, Birmingham Jewellery Quarter, & The Hawthorns. Birmingham Snow Hill has direct connection with Birmingham Moor Street, and is a ten minute walk from New Street station.

By car: The tramway runs for 22km from the centre of Birmingham to Wolverhampton. Car parking is difficult in the city centres. However, it is possible to park at stops along the route. The Hawthorns and Priestfield stops have park and ride facilities.

Description

This is one of the new British tramway systems. The tramway uses cars built by Firema, in Caserta, Italy. Most of the running is on reserved track (former railway tracks), though the highlight of any visit must be the street running from Priestfield to Wolverhampton, St Georges. As well as the street running section it is also possible to get close to the line for photography between Trinity Way and Black Lake (six stops) where a public footpath runs alongside the track. The depot is alongside Wednesbury, Great Western Street stop, but there is no public access. There are plans to build extensions to Brierley Hill and in the centre of Birmingham, but no work has yet started on these.

Tickets

Following the failure of the ticket machines at the stops the tramway has introduced conductors on the tramcars. Single, return and one day tickets for the trams are all available from the conductors. There are a variety of other day tickets

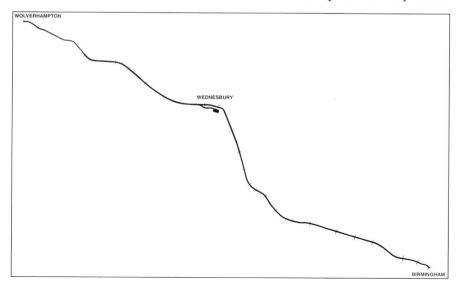

depending on the time you buy and whether you want to include local rail and all buses (Centrocard before 9.30am and Daytripper after 9.30am) or just West Midlands Travel buses and the Metro (Daysaver). These need to be purchased from railway stations or from West Midlands Travel Offices (there is one at New Street Station). If you travel to Birmingham by main line railway it is cheapest to purchase an "add on" all day ticket for West Midland Travel buses which is also valid on the Metro (note it only operates on the day of travel to Birmingham and is only available from certain railway stations. Check before travel as pre-purchase may be required).

Fleet
6 axle, single deck articulated Ansoldo Type 69, totally enclosed, built 1998

01	04	07	09	11	13	15
02	05	08	10	12	14	16
03	06					

Nearby
The Black Country Museum with its operating tramway is in Dudley, while the Aston Manor Road Transport Museum and Birmingham and Midland Museum Transport at Wythall are all worth a visit.

NOTTINGHAM EXPRESS TRANSIT (NET)

Address
NET Project Team
Lawrence House
Talbot Street
Nottingham
NG1 5NT
Tel: 0115 915 6600
Web: www.nottinghamcity.gov.uk
GR: SK585395
Gauge: 4' 8½"

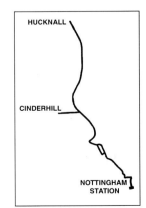

Open
All year.

How to get there
By public transport: There is a direct rail interchange at the following stations: Nottingham Midland, Bulwell and Hucknall.

Gleaming in the sunlight the new Nottingham trams show off their streamlined design.

By car: Parking in the city centre is difficult. There are park and ride facilities at Hucknall; Wilkinson Street; The Forest and Phoenix Park. The latter is recommended. Leave the M1 at junction 26 and take the A610 towards Nottingham. You will come to a roundabout, continue on the A610 to the next set of traffic lights. Turn left into the park and ride area. The tram stop is by the parking area.

Description

This is the newest of the British tramways having opened in the Autumn of 2003. The tramway runs for 11km from the centre of Nottingham to Hucknall, with a small spur from Highbury Vale to Phoenix Park. Most of the tramway runs on reserved track, but there is street-running from Wilkinson Street (where the depot is, no public access) to the city centre. The tramway is unusual in having a section where the two tracks are separated and run in different roads. This is between Wilkinson Street and The Forest.

Tickets

Tickets are sold on the trams by conductors or during busy periods at busy stops from conductors at the stop. There is a day ticket called "Tramrider" at £2. It appears there is an add-on fare of £2 for rail travellers (purchase when buying rail ticket from any UK railway station) that gives all-day travel. Those arriving by car will want to use the park and ride facilities where parking is free for tram users. The Wilkinson Street park and ride is next to the depot and has 900 parking places.

My favourite cliff lift, called the inclined tramway, is at Saltburn. It has been restored to its Victorian splendour.

Fleet

6 axle, five section, single deck articulated, totally enclosed, Adtranz Incentro trams built 2002/3.

201	204	206	208	210	212	214
202	205	207	209	211	213	215
203						

NET have announced that they will be naming all their trams. The actual process of putting names on the trams has not started. But some names have been selected: "Mavis Worthington", "Dinah Minton", "Erica Beardsmore", "D.H. Lawrence", "Sir Jesse Boot", "Lord Byron", "William Booth", "Bendigo Thompson" and "Robin Hood".

Nearby

The Crich Tramway Village is 15 miles to the west.

SALTBURN INCLINED TRAMWAY

Address

Saltburn Inclined Tramway
Lower Promenade
Saltburn
TS12 2QX

Tel: 01287 622528
GR: NZ666217
Gauge: 4' 8½"

Open

Daily between mid March and mid-September, then weekends mid-September to October.

How to get there

By public transport: travel by rail to Saltburn station. From the station walk a short distance ahead, then left into the old station building, and then through the shopping precinct to Milton Street. Turn right and walk along Milton Street, then turn left into Amber Street. At the end of Amber Street cross Marine Parade and turn right, walking along the promenade. The top of the inclined tramway is on your left.

By car: Saltburn is about ten miles east of Middlesborough on the A174. From the west drive through Saltburn to the top of a hill. Here bear left off the A170 into Marine Parade. There is on-street parking on this road. The top station of the inclined tramway is set slightly below the promenade of Marine Parade. The easiest way to find it is to look over the edge to the pier, the tramway being like an inland extension of the pier.

Description

In the 1860's Saltburn wanted to set itself up as a seaside resort to rival all the other famous Victorian resorts. However, this was not to be, and as a consequence it retains a charm of its own and I was captivated by it. The cliff tramway is in excellent order and on my visit the pier was being entirely rebuilt as a millennium project. The inclined tramway was built in 1884 and has always operated on the water counterbalance system. Indeed the informative leaflet on the tramway says that it is probably the world's oldest water balance lift. Apart from essential replacement work, the tramway is very much as originally built. The carriages have a Victorian charm enhanced by stained glass decoration to the windows. The twin tracks are 207ft long and 4' 2½" gauge. A short walk east from the lower station (across the A174) are the Italian Gardens with a 680 yard long 15" gauge miniature railway that operates in school holiday afternoons except Mondays.

Tickets

Single tickets only, sold at lower station.

Nearby

Saltburn is somewhat isolated. The cliff railways at Scarborough are around 35 miles along the coast to the south and the North of England Open Air Museum at Beamish is a similar distance north west.

SCARBOROUGH CLIFF LIFTS

Address

Tourist Information Centre
Unit 3
Pavilion House,
Valley Bridge Road
Scarborough
YO11 1UZ

Tel:	01723 361459 (South Cliff) and 01723 501754 (Central Cliff)	
GR:	South Cliff	TA045877
	St Nicholas Cliff	TA044883
	Central Cliff	TA044884
Gauge:	4ft 8½in for the South and Central cliffs.	
	7ft 6in for the St Nicholas cliff.	

Originally steam operated and now driven by an electric motor, the Central funicular at Scarborough links the upper town with the promenade.

The South Cliff funicular at Scarborough was the first to be built in Britain.

The St Nicholas funicular at Scarborough has the most spectacular position.

Open

Daily between Easter and mid-October, then weekends mid-October to Christmas.

How to get there

By public transport: travel by rail to Scarborough station. From here turn right into Westborough Way into the pedestrian-only central shopping area. Turn right into Vernon Road, then left into Falconer Road. At the end of Falconer Road you will see the top station for the Central Cliff Railway, just past the corner café. Ride down the railway. At the bottom turn right, and the St. Nicholas Cliff Railway is 100 yards on the right. The South Cliff Railway is further along the promenade, just past the Spa Complex.

By car: Scarborough is easy to find. Once in the town you will need to park in one of the many car parks. Scarborough has two beaches, the North Bay and the South Bay. All the cliff railways are on the South Bay. So walk to the South Bay Promenade. The Central Cliff Railway is about halfway along the beach, St. Nicholas is a hundred yards to the south, and the South Cliff Railway is at the southern edge of the beach. All are easily found and within comfortable walking distance of each other.

Description

All three cliff railways are electrically driven and have two carriages running on twin tracks. The South Cliff Railway has the distinction of being the first cliff railway to be built in Britain. Constructed in 1875 it has two 4' 8½" gauge tracks and is 284ft long. Originally using the water balance principle, the railway was converted to electrical operation in 1935. The St. Nicholas Cliff Railway is the youngest of the three, being built in 1930. It has twin 7' 6" gauge tracks which are each 103ft long. The lower stop is unusual as the traveller steps directly from the public pavement into the carriage – there is no station as such. The Central Cliff Lift is much older, having been built in 1880 and unusually was originally steam powered. Electrically driven since 1920, the two carriages ride on twin 4' 8½" gauge tracks each 234ft long. The cliff railways are owned by Scarborough Corporation, but appear to be seen solely as revenue earners. There are no leaflets or booklets about the railways, and the historical significance of the South Cliff Railway is only indicated by a small information sheet made by the staff and stuck on a window. The fourth cliff lift at North Cliff was closed relatively recently because it failed to show a profit, and now no sign of its existence remains. The infrastructure was purchased by Launceston and was transported to Cornwall.

Tickets

Single tickets only, sold at both top and bottom stations.

Nearby
Scarborough is also somewhat isolated. The inclined tramway at Saltburn is around 35 miles along the coast to the north and the Streetlife Museum at Hull is a similar distance south.

SEATON TRAMWAY

Address
	Harbour Road
	Seaton
	Devon
	EX12 2NQ
Tel:	01297 20375
Web:	www.tram.co.uk
GR:	SY246905
Gauge:	2' 9"

Open
Daily Easter to end October: Saturdays and Sundays November to mid-December and other days in February and March, contact the tramway for details.

Three new tramcars have been built for the Seaton Tramway. Here numbers 9 and 10 are being fitted out in the depot.

How to get there

By public transport: travel by rail to Axminster. Outside the station there is a bus service to Seaton. The bus trip takes about half an hour.

By car: From Junction 28 of the M5 take the A373 to Honiton. Follow signs for A35 to Axminster. At Axminster take A353 to Seaton. After nearly 4 miles there is a cross roads. Go across to B3172 to Seaton. At Seaton outskirts follow road to Town Centre. Just before the town centre the tramway terminus is on the right by Harbour Road Car Park (payment required).

Description

The Seaton Tramway was, quite rightly, awarded the South West small visitor attraction of the year for 2003. The tramway runs along the bed of an old railway for three miles from Seaton, via Colyford to Colyton. The round trip takes about an hour and for much of the run there are fine views over the River Axe and its wildlife. The tramway has its origins in North London when Claude Lane built a portable 15" gauge tramway that was taken to local fêtes. A wish for a more permanent home took Claude to St Leonards, Rhyl and Eastbourne before the trams came to a settled home at Seaton.

The period style terminus at Seaton superbly complements the tramcars, most of which have been built by the tramway staff. At Colyton the terminus is the old railway station, within a short walk from the centre of the village. There are souvenir shops at both termini and a cafe at Colyton. Parking is free at Colyton, but there are charges in the municipal car park at Seaton. Tram driving lessons are available as half or full-day courses on Fridays or Saturdays, pre-booking is essential.

Tickets

Purchase single, return, one day, two day or three day rover tickets before riding from Seaton ticket office (at the tram terminus) or Colyton station. Special arrangements are available for passengers boarding at Colyford – see the conductor.

Fleet

Maximum traction bogie, open top, unvestibuled, based on MET Type A, built 1964

   2

Maximum traction bogie, single deck, open boat, built 1961

   4

Maximum traction bogie, open top, vestibuled, built 1954, 1958 & 1968, rebuilt on various dates

   6*   7   8

* Originally built as a toastrack bogie single deck tramcar.

Equal wheel bogie, open top, vestibuled, built by Bolton Trams and Seaton Tramway 2002/3

    9   10   11

Equal wheel bogie, open top, vestibuled, built 1966, rebuilt 1980 and 1999

    12 (Originally built as an enclosed bogie single deck tramcar)

Maximum traction bogie, single deck, totally enclosed, built 1984 & 1992

    14 (using parts of MET 94) 16 (using parts of Bournemouth 106)

Maximum traction bogie, single deck, cross bench, adapted for disabled passengers, built 1988

    17

Reversed maximum traction bogie, single deck, totally enclosed, built 1998

    19 (using parts of Exeter 19, due to be given a new 3 axle chassis)

Works cars

Maximum traction bogie, mobile shop, built 1954, rebuilt 1960 and 1966

    01 (Withdrawn 1998, when new terminus at Seaton opened, now in store, no public access)

Maximum traction bogie, single deck, totally enclosed, works car, built 1969, rebuilt 1992

    02

Maximum traction bogie, welding trailer, built 1986, rebuilt with cover 1994

    03

Maximum traction bogie, Hydraulic hoist trailer, built 1988

    04

Four wheel, dropside works trailer, built 1988

    05

Four wheel, generator trailer, built 1992

    06

Maximum traction bogie trailer, framework only, awaiting completion

    No number (parked on siding at Colyford)

0-4-0 Ruston and Hornsby diesel non working parked at Colyton

    No number

Nearby

There is nothing within easy travelling distance, so just relax and enjoy the tramway for the whole day.

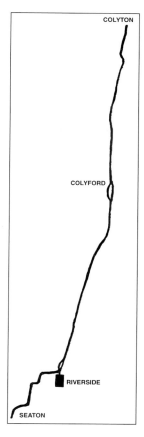

Another delightful funicular is at Shipley Glen. It retains all its Victorian charms.

SHIPLEY GLEN CABLE TRAMWAY

Address

Shipley Glen Cable Tramway
Prod Lane
Baildon
Nr Saltaire
Shipley
Bradford

Tel: 01274 589010 (recorded message) (www.glentramway.co.uk)
GR: SE140384
Gauge: 1' 8"

Open

January/February Sundays only; March/April Weekends and Easter Bank Holiday;
May-August Weekends and Bank Holidays; September/November Weekends only;
December Sundays only.

How to get there

By public transport: the nearest railway station is at Saltaire, which is the wrong side of the river. However, close by there is a footbridge across the river. The tramway is signposted and about 200 yards walk from the station.

By car: The tramway is in the woods on the opposite side of the river from Saltaire Village. From the end of the M606 take the Bradford Ring Road, A6177 right to drive around Bradford reaching the A6037 to Shipley. Then take the A6038 out of Shipley passing over a canal and the river. Immediately over the river look for Green Lane on the left. Turn into it and this leads to Coach Road. After a short drive there is a school on the right with a large circular roadway next to it. Park here. Walk on the path from the road towards the woods. The tramway will be found at the start of the woods. The 386 yard tramway saves a very stiff walk up the hill.

Description

This is a unique tramway. Built in 1895 by a Victorian entrepreneur as a means of getting the public up to his fairground at the top of Shipley Glen the tramway has somehow survived for over 100 years. In 1981 it closed and was restored and reopened in 1982 by the Bradford Trolleybus Association, who operated it until 1994. With the support of the Association the lease was then transferred to Mike Leak (a member of the BTA). He and his wife Maureen have been operating the tramway ever since, along with other volunteers. The income from the fares hardly covers the day-to-day maintenance, and major improvements have to be funded from other sources, including personal contributions. The tramway is always seeking new volunteers, and would welcome any readers of this book who can spare time to help on the tramway. It is a funicular as the four tramcars are permanently fixed in pairs which are bolted to the ends of the cable. The trams counterbalance each other. The 386 yard 1' 8" gauge tramway saves a very stiff walk up the hill. There is a museum and shop with souvenirs etc.

Tickets

Purchase tickets from the Shop/Museum at the top or the ticket office at the bottom of the tramway.

Fleet

Four cars permanently connected in pairs, 4 wheel, single deck, toastrack, built 1955.

No numbers.

Nearby

The Industrial Museum at Bradford is a couple of miles distance.

Number 1 in the Snaefell fleet at the summit outside the restaurant.

SNAEFELL MOUNTAIN TRAMWAY

Address
>   Isle of Man Transport
>   Transport Headquarters
>   Banks Circus
>   Douglas
>   Isle of Man
>   IM1 5PY

Tel: 01624 663366
GR: SC43427847
Gauge: 3' 6"

Open
Daily Easter to September.

How to get there
By public transport: For the tram enthusiast there is only one way, by electric tram from Douglas to Laxey.

By car: If you have taken your car over to the island and insist on not going by tram, drive to Laxey; there is parking by the tram stop.

Description

Another one of the Isle of Man's Victorian transport treasures. The mountain tramway was originally built using the centre Fell rail for braking purposes. When the tramcars were refitted with more powerful motors and full rheostatic braking around 1980, it was found that the Fell rail was no longer needed, though it is still in situ in case of emergency. The steep line uses only adhesion to climb the island's highest mountain. From the top, in good weather, it is possible to see England, Scotland, Wales and Ireland, as well as the whole of the island. The line is nearly five miles long and has a gauge of 3' 6", so is not compatible with the Manx Electric. At Laxey the Snaefell line runs alongside the Manx Electric. There is an exchange siding where Snaefell cars are mounted on temporary Manx Electric bogies to be towed to Derby Castle for maintenance and repairs. At the top of Snaefell there is a restaurant and souvenir shop.

Tickets

Single or return tickets are sold at the ticket office at Laxey or from the conductor if boarding at Bungalow or the summit. For one day, three day and seven day tickets, see details under Manx Electric Railway.

Fleet

Bogie, single deck, totally enclosed, built 1895.

<u>   1   </u>   2   <u>   3   </u>   4   5*   <u>   6   </u>

* Rebuilt 1971 after a fire and rebuilt 1998/99 for disabled access with power lift.

Freight and Service Vehicles

Bogie, single deck, double cab locomotive "Maria", replica, built 1996.

   7*

* Remains of original car 7 lie alongside the shed.

4 wheel, open wagon, built 1981 & 1982.

   1   2

Ex-Civil Aviation Authority Railcar, unserviceable stored on site, built 1977.

   1

Civil Aviation Authority Railcar, no public access, built 1977 & 1991.

   3   4

Route map – see Manx Electric Railway.

Nearby

The Manx Electric Railway connects with the mountain railway at Laxey. In Douglas there is the Douglas Horse Tramway, also in Douglas is the Manx Museum, while across the island in Peel is the Manx Transport Museum.

The future of the Southend cliff lift is in doubt as a new vertical lift is being built nearby.

SOUTHEND CLIFF RAILWAY

Address

Southend Tourist Information Centre
Civic Centre
Victoria Avenue
Southend
Essex
SS2 6ER

Tel: 01702 618899
GR: TQ881851
Gauge: 4' 6"

Open

Easter to September

How to get there

By public transport: travel by rail to Southend Central station. From here it is a short walk (less than half a mile) down the High Street to the Pier. Keep on the promenade and walk west towards Westcliff-on-Sea. The cliff railway is on the right (away from the sea) about 300 yards past the pier.

By car: from junction 29 of the M25 take the A127 to Southend, or the A13 from junction 30 of the M25. Once in Southend follow the signs to the Pier. Keep on the promenade heading west from the pier (towards Westcliff-on-Sea). The cliff railway is about 300 yards from the pier on the right hand side of the road (away from the sea).

Description

If you want to see the Southend Cliff Lift then get there soon. The Council is building a new vertical lift to connect the High Street with the Pier. This will make the funicular redundant and it is likely to be closed. However, even if you visit it, you may not be able to travel in it. On my recent visit it was out of action owing to a seized bearing. They were waiting for replacement parts, which were taking a long time, as they had to be specially made. I fear that the building of the new lift will overtake the repair of the funicular. It was built in 1912, has a single car running on a single track 130ft long with the car counterbalanced by a permanent counterweight running on a 1' 9" gauge track underneath.

Tickets

Single tickets are issued by the operator.

Nearby

You almost fall over the pier getting to the cliff railway. Do not miss out on the Pier Museum.

SOUTHEND PIER TRAMWAY

Address

　　　　Southend Pier Railway
　　　　Southend Pier
　　　　Southend-on-Sea
　　　　Essex
GR:　　TQ894846
Gauge:　3' 0"

Open

All year.

How to get there

By public transport: travel by rail to Southend Central station. From here it is a short walk (less than half a mile) down the High Street to the Pier.

A rare view of the bogie flat wagon in use. It is carrying equipment to the pier end.

By car: From Junction 29 of the M25 take the A127 to Southend, or the A13 from Junction 30 of the M25. Once in Southend follow the signs to the Pier. There is some metered parking along the promenade. At the pier head go down the steps to the Pier Train station.

Description

It is remarkable that the Southend Pier and its railway have survived. In 1976 there was a major fire at the pier head causing severe damage. In the subsequent years the Council decided that the tramway was life-expired and closed it in 1978. The future of both the tramway and the pier was in the balance. In 1982 all the trams and ancillary equipment were sold for scrap. However, in 1985 the Council appointed contractors to rebuild the tramway using 3' 0" gauge track on new hard-wood decking. The new trams consist of two seven car diesel units using hydraulic drive. The tramway goes along the 1.25 mile longest pier in the world. Recently the Council has rebuilt the Pier Entrance in a modern design, with plenty of glass. Whilst smart and clean the design is at odds with the Victorian/Edwardian heritage of the pier. While on the pier a visit to the Southend Pier Museum is recommended as some of the earlier electric trams are on display. The museum is situated near the landward terminus of the tramway.

Tickets

Entry to the pier can be for walking only, walking one way and a single trip on the train, or a return train trip. The upper ticket office sells tickets for walking or walking out and riding back. The lower ticket office, by the train station, sells tickets for a ride out and walk back or return trips on the tram.

Fleet

7 car diesel hydraulic unit, single deck, totally enclosed, built 1986.
   A "Sir John Betjeman"   B "Sir William Heygate"
6 wheel battery railcar for winter passenger service, built 1996.
   1835
One, bogie goods vehicle, flat wagon, no number

Nearby

Do not miss out on the Pier Museum; the entrance is at the same level as the station. Also nearby is the Southend funicular and a little further along at Leigh is the Lynne Tait Gallery with a Southend Pier carriage.

Number 122 rides past the Hillsborough Barracks on its way to Meadowhall.

SOUTH YORKSHIRE SUPERTRAM (SHEFFIELD)

Address
    Stagecoach Supertram Ltd
    The Nunnery
    Woodburn Road
    Sheffield
    S9 3LS
Tel: 0114 275 9888. **Travel Line:** 0114 276 7575
Travel Line: 0114 276 7575
GR: SK370884
Gauge: 4' 8½"

Open
All year.

How to get there
By public transport: travel by rail to Sheffield Midland station. Follow the signs to the tram stop alongside the station.
By car: I find the easiest access is off Junction 34 of the M1 and heading for the

Meadowhall Shopping Complex. There is a Park and Ride facility at the Meadowhall Interchange, which is on the northern side of the shopping complex. There is also Park and Ride beside the depot (on the Meadowhall route by Sheffield Parkway or Cricket Inn Road stop). Travel into the city centre is best by tram.

Description

The 15 miles of new tramway started operation in 1994 and was fully opened in 1995. There is a mixture of street running (in the city centre and the Middlewood and Malin Bridge routes) and reserved track (in the suburbs). The route out to Halfway is distinctly rural for its later part with the trams running alongside farm fields. One favourite place for photographers is by the bowstring arch bridge (nearest stop Fitzalan Square). There is pedestrian access onto the bridge and this leads to the double track triangle linking all the routes. As much of the city centre tramway runs along the same streets as the old tramway comparisons can be made with old photographs. The depot (no public access) is at Nunnery stop.

Tickets

Following the heavy vandalisation of the ticket machines at the stops, conductors

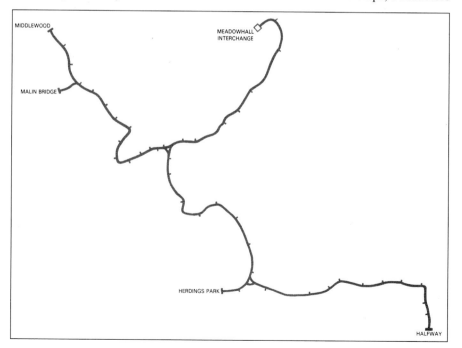

have been placed on the trams. They will sell you single, return and one day tickets. The park and ride facilities include a one-day ticket in with the parking cost and represent good value to money.

Fleet
8 axle, single deck articulated, totally enclosed, built 1993 & 1994.

101	105	109	113	117	120	123
102	106	110	114	118	121	124
103	107	111	115	119	122	125
104	108	112	116			

Nearby
Nottingham NET is about 35 miles south down the M1 while Manchester Metrolink is about the same distance to the west.

STANSTED AIRPORT PEOPLE MOVER

Address
British Airports Authority
Stansted Airport
Essex

Tel: 01279 663725 or 0870 0000 303
GR: TL550240
Gauge: Rubber tyres on concrete track

Open
All year.

How to get there
Public transport: Travel by rail to Stansted Airport Station.
By car: From Junction 8 of the M11 follow the signs to the airport.

Description
This is an unusual form of public transport in that it is limited to passengers actually flying out of or into the airport and then it is compulsory to travel on it! Passengers flying out of the airport pass through the usual emigration and security checks to a departures lounge in the main terminal building. Then to get to some embarkation gates (new gates have been opened recently where the people mover is not used) it is necessary to travel on the people mover. Small carriages, operating as single units or in pairs, carry passengers to the outer terminal gates. The

operation is fully automatic. The carriages are electrically driven and run on rubber tyres with a centrally mounted guide-way, which incorporates the power supply. At the main terminal building there are two stops. The first disembarks arriving passengers by the emigration and baggage halls, the other to pick up departing passengers to take them to their gates. As much of the track is underground the system is not visible from any non-passenger area of the airport. There is no photograph, because when I took my camera out to get a picture I was pounced on and told firmly that no photography is allowed in the airport. I felt it best not to argue as I did want to catch my flight.

Tickets
Having purchased your flight the journey on the people mover is free.

Fleet
2 axle, single deck, totally enclosed.

1	3	5	7	8	9	10
2	4	6				

Nearby
London is about 35 miles south down the M11.

TORQUAY, BABBACOMBE CLIFF RAILWAY

Address
Babbacombe Cliff Railway
Babbacombe
Torquay
Devon

Tel: 01803 328750
GR: SX925656
Gauge: 5' 8"

Open
Good Friday to September inclusive

How to get there
By public transport: travel by rail to Torquay station. From here catch a bus to Babbacombe or St. Marychurch. Ask for either north end of Babbacombe Downs or the Model Village. The upper station of the cliff railway is tucked behind a café which is at the north end of the Babbacombe Downs. The cliff railway itself travels

from Babbacombe to Oddicombe Beach and is sometimes referred to under that name.

By car: from the end (junction 31) of the M5 head on the A38 towards Exeter. After a couple of miles take the A380 to Torquay. After 12 miles leave the A380 and follow the signs to Torquay. Look for signs to St. Marychurch at traffic lights. Turn left and follow the road straight on until it ends at the T junction in St. Marychurch. Turn right towards Babbacombe. A little further on there are signs to the cliff railway, turn left and note the café in front of you. Find on-street parking (busy during the season due to the Model Village). Walk back to the café and follow the footpath on its right hand side. Turn left behind the café and the upper station of the cliff lift comes into sight.

Description

Opened in 1926, this is one of the younger cliff railways. However, it is also amongst the longest with 716ft of 5' 8" gauge track. The cars are also the fastest that I have travelled on, taking 1½ minutes for the journey at a speed of 500ft per minute. The electrically operated cars have almost entirely standing room only, with four small seats, one in each corner. Each car can carry up to 40 passengers at a time, and with the popularity of the fairly isolated Oddicombe beach with holiday makers, the cliff railway needs to be able to move large numbers of people quickly. Near the top station of the lift is Babbacombe Model Village. Turn right and walk down the road. The Model Village is at the end of the road. It has an oper-

The Babbacombe cliff lift taking holiday makers to Oddicombe beach.

ating model funicular as part of the display.

Tickets
Single and return purchased at either station.

Nearby
The cliff railway is rather isolated. The Seaton Tramway is about 40 miles along the coast to the east and Launceston Steam Railway the same distance to the west.

TYNE AND WEAR METRO

Address
Nexus
Cuthbert House
All Saints
Newcastle upon Tyne
NE1 2DA
Tel: 0191 203 3333. **Travel Line:** 0870 608 2 608
Web: www.tyneandwearmetro.co.uk

Another great success has been the Tyne and Wear Metro. The system has been extended and now serves a large area around Newcastle and Gateshead. Photograph David Cole.

GR: NZ250643
Gauge: 4' 8½"
Open
All year.

How to get there
By public transport: travel by rail to Newcastle Central station. The underground Metro station is below the railway station, just follow the signs.
By car: The Metro runs in a large loop from Newcastle City Centre to Tynemouth and Whitley Bay and back to the city centre. There are also two branches, one North West to the airport, and the other across the River Tyne to South Shields. With a system as extensive as this you can take your choice. Car parking is indicated at Walkergate, Tynemouth, Whitley Bay, Shire Moor, Benton, Four Lane Ends, Regent Centre, Kingston Park, Bank Foot, Callerton Parkway, Heworth and Jarrow stations.

Description
This was the first of the new technology light rail systems to be built in Britain. It has many railway characteristics such as high platforms and entirely reserved track, while the vehicles themselves are very light rail, working off a DC overhead system. The first part of the system opened in 1980 while the most recent extension, to the airport, opened in 1991. Currently there are around 37 route miles with 58 stations. Tickets are sold from machines inside each station entrance. Day

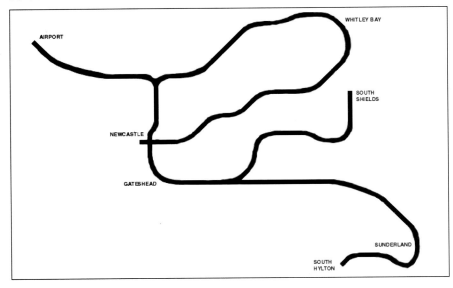

tickets are available called "DaySaver". The machines only accept change – they do not take notes. So make sure you have plenty of coins.

Tickets
Single and return tickets are sold by machines at each stop.

Fleet
6 axle, single deck articulated, totally enclosed, built 1978 – 1981.

4001	4014	4027	4040	4053	4066	4079
4002	4015	4028	4041#	4054	4067	4080
4003	4016	4029	4042	4055	4068	4081
4004	4017	4030	4043	4056	4069	4082
4005	4018	4031	4044	4057	4070	4083
4006	4019	4032	4045	4058	4071	4084
4007	4020	4033	4046	4059	4072	4085
4008	4021	4034	4047	4060	4073	4086
4009	4022	4035	4048	4061	4074	4087
4010	4023	4036	4049	4062	4075	4088
4011	4024	4037	4050	4063	4076	4089
4012	4025	4038	4051	4064	4077~	4090
4013	4026*	4039	4052	4065+	4078>	

* "George Stephenson"   # "Harry Cowans"   + "Dame Catherine Cookson"
~ "Robert Stephenson"   > "Ellen Wilkinson".

Works Locomotives
0-4-0 Battery Electric locomotives, built 1989 – 1990.

BL1   BL2   BL3

Nearby
The North of England Open Air Museum at Beamish is about 6 miles from Newcastle city centre.

VOLKS ELECTRIC RAILWAY, BRIGHTON

Address
Volks Electric Railway
Madeira Drive
Brighton
East Sussex
Tel: 01273 292718
Web: www.volkselectricrailway.co.uk

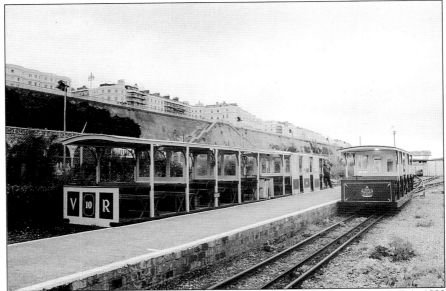

The world's oldest operating electric tramway is in Brighton. Built by Magnus Volk in 1883 it is still running after more than 120 years.

GR: TQ315039
Gauge: 2' 8½"

Open
Easter to September.

How to get there
By public transport: travel by rail to Brighton station. Volk's railway is about 1.5 miles; walk down Queen's Road, turn left into Church Street to the Brighton Pavilion. Go past the front of the Pavilion to Palace Pier. The railway is 200 yards further along Madeira Drive.

By car: From the end of the M23 (Junction 11) take the A23 to Brighton. In Brighton follow signs to Brighton Pavilion. When at the Pavilion take the road to the sea front. At the roundabout by the pier take Madeira Drive, along the sea front. Volks Electric Railway is on the right, running alongside the road. Metered parking is available along the front.

Description
Volks Electric Railway was the first public electric railway to be opened in Britain. It opened in 1883 on a 2' 0" gauge track, using an unusual two rail electrical

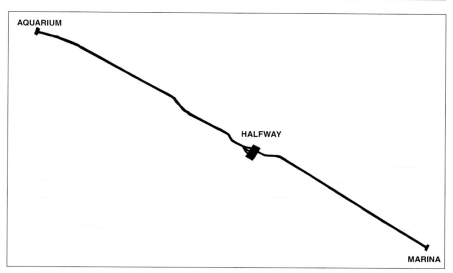

supply. In 1884 an extension was opened to the gauge of 2' 8½" and the original line changed to the new gauge, which the line continues to have. Over recent years the line has been allowed to deteriorate more than is worthy for such a historic monument. The Volks Electric Railway Society is doing a good job supporting the pioneer railway and helping the Council to maintain the line and the stock. The depot (no public access) is at the halfway point, by the fairground. Near by at Paston Place and built into the rock face of the cliff below Marine Parade is the Office and Workshop. This was Magnus Volk's original office and he would stand on the balcony checking that the line was running properly. He would be pleased to know that his railway has now become the oldest operating electric railway in the world.

If the tide is low take the opportunity to go to the seashore between the new marina and Rottingdean. Access is by foot alongside the marina or by car by parking on Marine Drive the other side of the marina. There are steps down the cliff to the beach. Below high tide mark can be seen some large concrete blocks, sited roughly in pairs and making two lines parallel to the cliff. These are the 'sleepers' from the long-gone Brighton and Rottingdean Seashore Electric Tramroad, with its 'Daddy Long Legs' tramcar which travelled in the sea at high tide. Well worth a visit.

Tickets

Single and return tickets are sold at the ticket offices at Aquarium, Halfway and Marina.

Fleet

The railway renumbered its fleet in 1999 so that the tramcars carry, as far as possible, the original numbers allocated to them by Magnus Volk.
4 wheel, single deck, semi open, unvestibuled, built 1892 & 1901.

| 3 | 4 | 6 | 7 | 8 |

4 wheel, single deck, crossbench, unvestibuled, built 1910.

9

4 wheel, single deck, crossbench, unvestibuled, ex-Southend Pier, in store, no public access, built 1898.

9

4 wheel, single deck, crossbench, unvestibuled, built 1926.

10

4 wheel works diesel shunter, built 1987.

40D530 (Works Number)

Nearby

Hastings with its two cliff railways is about 35 miles along the coast to the east.

TRAMWAY MUSEUMS AND HERITAGE TRAMWAYS IN THE BRITISH ISLES

Museums included in this section are those with either an operating tramway or with static tramcar(s) on display. Single tramcars can be traced from the list of Historic Tramcars in Section 3. Most museums have an entrance charge.

ALFORD VALLEY RAILWAY

Address

Alford Valley Railway
Alford Station
Alford
Aberdeenshire

Tel: 01975 562326
GR: NJ582162
Gauge: 2' 0"

Open

Daily June, July and August. Weekends only April, May and September.

How to get there

By public transport: the nearest railway station is at Aberdeen, some 25 miles away. Outside the station is the bus station. Here take a Bluebird coach to Alford. At Alford alight at the Vale Hotel bus stop, which is the nearest to the railway.
By car: Alford is approximately 25 miles west of Aberdeen on the A944. Alford Valley Railway is based at the former GNSR Alford Station.

Description

Strictly speaking this is a narrow gauge (2 feet) railway rather than a heritage tramway. However the railway uses a restored Aberdeen tramcar body as a coach. The tramcar is believed to be number 11 built in 1911 for the Aberdeen Suburban Tramways Company, although the railway advertises it as being of 1895 vintage. It was originally a balcony top, vestibuled, standard gauge, four wheel tramcar. It was withdrawn and sold on the closure of the tramway in 1927. As it is running on the railway the lower saloon of the tramcar has been restored, there is no upper deck, and railway style platforms have been fitted. There are no motors or controllers. In place of the standard gauge truck there are two 2 feet gauge bogies.

Tram on display

System	No.	Built	Description
Aberdeen	11	1911	4 wheel, balcony top, vestibuled, restored as single deck trailer.

Nearby
The Grampian Transport Museum, also in Alford.

ASTON MANOR ROAD TRANSPORT MUSEUM

Address
Aston Manor Road Transport Museum
The Old Tram Depot
208-216 Witton Lane
Witton
Birmingham
B6 6QE
Tel: 0121 322 2298 (24 hour information line)
GR: SP080904
Gauge: 3' 6"

Open
Saturdays, Sundays and Bank Holiday Mondays.

How to get there
By public transport: the nearest railway station is Witton; from here walk to the roundabout on Witton Road (within sight of station), turn left and the museum is on the left about 50 yards from the roundabout. Aston Station on the cross-city line is ¾ mile from the museum. Ask directions to Aston Villa Football ground, walk past the ground keeping it on your left, and the museum is at the far end of the ground on the opposite side of the road.

By car: From junction 6 of the M6 (spaghetti junction) follow signs for A38(M) City centre. Leave at the first slip road on left up to roundabout. Take right hand road (Victoria Road) to next roundabout. Take furthest right (B4140) to Witton. At next roundabout take right onto Witton Lane (alongside the Aston Villa football

Aston Manor in the days when the trams were running. Today the building is very recognisable as a tram depot. Photograph Ray Wilson, courtesy Tramway and Light Railway Society Archive.

ground). The museum is immediately on the left on entering Witton Lane. Free car park alongside museum.

Description

The museum building is a former tram depot for Birmingham Corporation Tramways. Opened originally for steam tram trailers, it was subsequently converted for electric trams. The original tram tracks and stone setts are still in situ in the depot. Most of the museum exhibits are buses and trolleybuses. For the tram enthusiast there is the TLRS National Model Tram Collection, a large scale operating model tramway, a small scale tramway layout operated by the public and the unrestored bodies of Birmingham and Bournemouth tramcars. In addition to the friendly staff there is a book and model shop and a cafe.

Trams on display

System	No.	Built	Description
Birmingham	107	1906	4 wheel, balcony top, vestibuled.

Nearby
The Midland Metro, Birmingham and Midland Museum Transport at Wythall and the Black Country Museum with its operating tramway in Dudley are all worth a visit.

BIRKENHEAD TRAMWAYS

Address
  Birkenhead Tramway
  Pacific Road
  Woodside Pier
  Birkenhead
  Merseyside
Details from Tourist Information Centre: 0151 647 6780
GR: SJ330838
Gauge: 4' 8½"

Open
The tramway operates afternoons Easter to October Tuesday to Saturday; closed Mondays except Bank Holidays. For winter operating times contact

Liverpool 762 has recently been fully restored and operates on the Birkenhead Heritage Tramway.

Birkenhead Tourist Information Centre.

How to get there

By public transport: travel by rail to Birkenhead, Hamilton Square station; turn left out of station and walk to Woodside Pier where the tram terminus is. Alternatively take the ferry from Liverpool which calls at Woodside Pier.
By car: From Junction 3 of the M53 take A552 towards Birkenhead. In Birkenhead follow signs to Woodside Pier. On-street parking is available close to the depot at the other end of the line.

Description

An operating tramway running from Woodside Pier (with ferry connections to Liverpool) along Shore Road to the working Egerton Bascule bridge and on to the depot in Taylor Street. It initially opened with two tramcars that were specially built in 1992 for Birkenhead by the Hong Kong Tramways Company. Now some superbly restored heritage tramcars are also in service. The trams are restored and maintained by the Merseyside Tramway Preservation Society.

Tickets

Tram tickets are sold in the Tourist Information Centre in Woodside Pier.

Trams on display or in collection

System	No.	Built	Description
Birkenhead	7	1876	Horse car, In Woodside Pier.
Birkenhead	20	1901	4 wheel, open top, unvestibuled.
Douglas	46	1908	Horse car, 4 wheel, crossbench.
Dundee	2	1882	Steam tram trailer (in store, no public access).
Hong Kong	69	1992	4 wheel, double deck, totally enclosed.
Hong Kong	70	1992	4 wheel, double deck, totally enclosed.
Liverpool	43	1890	Horse car, double deck, open top.
Liverpool	245	1938	4 wheel, double deck, totally enclosed.
Liverpool	762	1930	Bogie, double deck, totally enclosed.
Wallasey	78	1920	4 wheel, balcony top, vestibuled.

Nearby

The tramway is part of the Birkenhead Heritage Trail which includes the Wirral Museum, Shore Road Pumping Station, Egerton Bridge, Birkenhead Priory and St Mary's Tower and the Williamson Art Gallery and Museum. There are no other attractions to interest the tram enthusiast within easy travelling distance.

BIRMINGHAM AND MIDLAND MUSEUM OF TRANSPORT

Address

Birmingham and Midland Museum of Transport
Chapel Lane
Wythall
Birmingham
B47 6JX

Tel: 01564 826471
Web: www.bammot.org.uk
GR: SP074749
Gauge: 4' 8½"

Open

Operating days (write to museum for details) though the museum is open to casual visitors (not all facilities will be available) each Saturday and Sunday Easter to November.

How to get there

By public transport: the museum is not easy to get to. The nearest railway station is Wythall which is a 25 minute walk from the museum. On special Open Days vintage bus services are provided to the museum from Birmingham. Write to the museum for dates and details.

By car: From Junction 3 of the M42 go north (towards Birmingham) on the A435. At a large roundabout (with Beckets Farm on left) turn left. After a couple of hundred yards turn left into country road (signposted to the Transport Museum). Entrance to the Museum is on the right just before Wythall Church (disused).

Description

The transport museum is mainly for buses. There is a single tramcar in the collection from Frankfurt (a bogie single deck totally enclosed tramcar number 210). It is another example of a twinning present (Birmingham and Frankfurt are twinned) that has not been fully thought out. The tramcar has been stored outside and is exposed to the elements. It continues to rot gently. The plans to lay some track for operation are still unfulfilled.

Tram on display

System	No.	Built	Description
Frankfurt	210	1956	Bogie, single deck, totally enclosed.

Nearby
The Midland Metro and Aston Manor Road Transport Museums are in Birmingham while the Black Country Museum with its operating tramway is in Dudley.

BIRMINGHAM THINKTANK

Address
Birmingham Thinktank
Millennium Point
Curzon Street
Birmingham
B4 7XG
Tel: 0121 202 2333
GR: SP074749
Gauge: 3' 6"

Open
July to August every day.

How to get there
Public transport: Travel by rail to Moor Street Station, turn right out of the station and walk down the ramp turning right into Albert Street. Curzon Street is a continuation of Albert Street and the Millennium Centre is a massive building on the left, in total about half a mile from the station. If arriving at New Street Station, exit at the main concourse level and follow the signs to Moor Street. At Moor Street continue as above.

By car: From Junction 6 of the M6 (Spaghetti Junction) follow the signs to the city centre. Come off at the second fly-under on to the roundabout on the ring road A4540. Take the first left on the roundabout (A4540). Go past the traffic lights to the first roundabout, signposted to Thinktank at Millennium Point and take the right exit. Almost immediately turn left into Cardigan Street. At the end of the street turn right into Curzon Street. The Millennium Point and Thinktank is the big building on the right, with lots of (expensive) car parking.

Description

The old (free) Science Museum was closed in 2000 and its contents transferred to a new, high tech, Discovery Centre which opened a couple of years later. For the tram enthusiast the result has been spectacularly depressing. The new centre costs over £8.00 to enter on top of the extortionate car parking charges. The age of the tram is represented only by car 395 and a small picture display, the other tram related exhibits having been disposed of. The picture display shows photographs of London trams, describing them as Birmingham trams. The tram itself has not been cleaned since being in the old museum, so it is covered in dust and is aging badly. Quite frankly you would be better off spending the time at any of the other attractions around Birmingham. But if you do go, take a moment outside, turn to face away from the building and look across Curzon Street. The large old square building a block away was built in 1838 and was one of the first railway stations to serve Birmingham. It is the oldest surviving railway terminus building in the world that is still in its original location. Alas it is now no longer part of the railway network and stands rather forlornly next to a mail sorting centre.

Trams in collection

System	No.	Built	Description
Birmingham	395	1912	4 wheel, balcony top, vestibuled.

Nearby

The Midland Metro and Aston Manor Road Transport Museums are in Birmingham, the Black Country Museum with its operating tramway is in Dudley and the Birmingham and Midland Transport Museum is near Wythall.

Restored to its original condition Wolverhampton 49 takes its first run ready to carry passengers at the Black Country Museum.

BLACK COUNTRY LIVING MUSEUM, DUDLEY

Address

Black Country Living Museum
Tipton Road
Dudley
West Midlands DY1 4SQ
Tel: 0121 557 9643
Web: http://www.bclm.co.uk
GR: SO949912
Gauge: 3' 6"

Open

Every day March to October. Wednesday to Sunday November to February.

How to get there

By public transport: travel by train to Tipton station. Buses run past the museum from Owen Street opposite the station.
By car: From Junction 2 of the M5 take the Birmingham New Road (A4123) towards Wolverhampton. After 2 miles there is a roundabout, follow A4123 to

Wolverhampton. At next traffic lights turn left into Tipton Road, A4037. Entrance to large free car park for Museum is on right.

Description

This museum is on a 26 acre open-air site with many buildings from the Black Country re-erected to form a village (including its own licensed pub and consecrated church). The museum has been growing with additional items being brought to site. The tramway connects the entrance complex to the buildings forming the village. It is unique in this country as it is the only operating tramway which is to the Birmingham and Black Country gauge of 3ft 6in. The tramway is actively supported by the Black Country Museum Transport Group (see Societies) whose members will often be operating the tramcar. You will want to allow extra time to visit the other exhibits on the site including a mine and the restored shops, houses, church, pub and cinema. There is a 1920's chip shop (selling the best fish and chips in Britain) a cafe/restaurant and souvenir shop in the museum.

Trams on display or in collection

System	No.	Built	Description
Birmingham Central Tys	–	1888	Bogie Cable tram, in store no public access.
Dudley, Stourbridge & District	5	1920	4 wheel, single deck, totally enclosed.
Dudley, Stourbridge & District	75	1919	4 wheel, single deck, totally enclosed, under tarpaulins
Lisbon	361	1906	Bogie, single deck, totally enclosed.
Wolverhampton & District	19	1902	4 wheel, engineering car, under tarpaulins.
Wolverhampton & District	34	1919	4 wheel, single deck, totally enclosed.
Wolverhampton & District	102	1920	4 wheel, single deck, totally enclosed, used as shelter.
Wolverhampton Corp	49	1909	4 wheel, open top, unvestibuled.
Wolverhampton Tys Co	23	1892	Horse car, 4 wheel, double deck, open top.

Nearby

The Midland Metro and Aston Manor Road Transport Museums are in Birmingham and the Birmingham and Midland Transport Museum is near Wythall.

Blackpool 304, restored by the Lancastrian Transport Trust and on loan to Blackpool Tramways.

BLACKPOOL LANCASTRIAN TRANSPORT TRUST COLLECTION

Address

Lancastrian Transport Trust Workshop
Brinwell Road
Clifton Road Industrial Estate
Blackpool

Web: www.ltt.org.uk
GR: SD335340
Gauge: 4' 8½"

Open

Special open days only (write to Trust for details).

How to get there

Public transport: Travel by rail to Blackpool Station. Walk down Talbot Road to Talbot Square, by North Pier. In Market Street, parallel to the promenade, catch a number 6 bus for Mereside. Ask the driver to drop you at the Clifton Road Industrial Estate. On open days a free vintage bus service operates from Gynn

Square to the Workshop. From the station walk to the promenade and catch a northbound tram to Gynn Square.

By car: From junction 4 of the M55, the end, continue straight on to the first roundabout. Take the right exit into Ashworth Road. After 500 yards there is a 'T' junction on to Clifton Road. Turn left and then take the fourth left into Brinwell Road.

Description

The Lancastrian Transport Trust was set up to preserve public transport relevant to Blackpool and the surrounding area. It has a collection of buses and trams. The trams are available for the public to see on special open days.

Trams in collection

System	No.	Built	Description
Blackpool	8	1974	OMO car, in store no public access, rebuilt on 1935 Railcoach.
Blackpool	143	1924	Formerly works car 753, awaiting restoration to original "Standard" condition.
Blackpool	304	1952	Restored and on loan to Blackpool Tramways.
Blackpool	663	1953	Awaiting restoration.
Blackpool	732	1961	Illuminated Rocket tram, in store no public access, built on 1928 Pantograph car.

Nearby

Blackpool Tram system.

BRADFORD INDUSTRIAL MUSEUM

Address

Bradford Industrial Museum
Moorside Mills, Moorside Road
Bradford BD2 3HP

Tel: 01274 631756
GR: SE195379
Gauge: 4' 0"

Open

Tuesday-Sunday all year (closed Christmas Day, Boxing Day and Good Friday),
open other Bank Holiday Mondays.

How to get there

By public transport: Travel by rail to Bradford Interchange station. Take a bus
number 896 from Interchange Bus Station which travels past Moorside Road.
Alight at the Moorside Road stop and walk down Moorside Road to the museum.
By car: From Bradford city centre take the Harrogate Road (A658) after 2 to 3
miles the Museum is signposted. Turn right off A658 into Moorside Road.
Museum is 300 yards on left, free car park.

Description

In the museum grounds there is a short 4' 0" gauge horse tramway that operates
with replica horse car Bradford 40 (built in 1992 by W.G.H. Ltd). Operation
depends upon horse availability, and when raining only works for a limited time.
In the museum itself is Bradford 104 as a static exhibit. There are also some nice
models of former Bradford trams and the headlamp panels from three other tramcars. The museum is mainly devoted to the woollen mill machinery, although there
is a transport gallery with old cars and a small saddle tank steam locomotive.
Moorside House, the Mill Owner's home restored in period style, is worth a visit.
For a full day, combine this museum with a ride on the Shipley Glen Tramway.

Trams on display

System	No.	Built	Description
Bradford	40	1892	Replica horse car, 4 wheel, single deck, unvestibuled based on 1892 design.
Bradford	104	1925	4 wheel, balcony top, vestibuled.

The Industrial Museum in Bradford is home to number 104 and horse car 40.

Nearby

The Shipley Glen Tramway at Saltaire is well worth a visit.

BRISTOL AERO COLLECTION

Address

Bristol Aero Collection
Hanger 1A
Kemble Airfield
Nr Cirencester
Glos
GL7 6BA

Tel: 01285 771204
GR: ST960960
Gauge: 4' 8½"

Open

Good Friday, Easter Saturday, Sunday and Monday. Every Sunday middle April to end October and Bank Holiday Mondays.

How to get there

Public transport: Travel by rail to Kemble. The museum is a brisk walk from the station.
By car: From junction 17 of the M4 take the A429 north towards Malmesbury and Cirencester. Carry on the A429 past Malmesbury. About six miles further on the airfield is on the left.

Description

An Aero Collection is a strange entry in this book, but it qualifies because it has a Bristol horse tram in the collection, although I understand it never flew. The tramcar was built in 1895 and makes an unusual exhibit. It is currently under restoration, but still on display.

Tram on display

System	No.	Built	Description
Bristol	98-115 series	1895	Horse car, 4 wheel, open top, unvestibuled.

Nearby
The Clifton Rocks Railway is about 30 miles south west and the Milestones Museum, Basingstoke is around 50 miles south east.

CEFN COED COLLIERY MUSEUM

Address
Cefn Coed Colliery Museum
Crynant
Neath
SA10 8SN
Tel: 01639 750556
GR: SN790046
Gauge: 4' 8½"

Open
Daily April-October; Pre booked groups November-March

How to get there
By public transport: travel by rail to Neath station. From the station walk to the one-way system of roads surrounding the shopping centre. Catch a number 158 bus with the destination 'Banwen'. Ask to be put off at the bus stop at the museum in Crynant. For timetable and up-to-date information contact South Wales Transport 01792 475511.
By car: From Junction 43 of the M4 take the A465 towards Neath. Stay on the A465 bypassing Neath, about three miles north of Neath take the left turn on

Possibly the only remaining gas powered tram in the world can be found at Cefn Coed Museum.

the A4109 (the museum is signposted at this junction). After another three miles the museum is found on the left. Drive past the museum to find the car park.

Description

The museum is devoted to the heritage of the mining industry in South Wales. There is a walk through underground mine which illustrates the different mining techniques used through the years. Then you can inspect the machinery in the winding house. It is in this building where you can find the tramway interest. Neath was one of the rare systems using gas powered trams. A solitary example of the tramcar fleet has survived and has been restored to static exhibit state. The museum claims that it is the only surviving gas tramcar in the world, so it is worth a visit to see this unique tramcar. One word of caution, the tramcar is displayed at a lower level than the rest of the building. Access is down a staircase and there is very little space around it. If you want to take photographs you will need a wide angle lens.

Tram on display

System	No.	Built	Description
Neath	1	1896	4 wheel open top, unvestibuled

Nearby

The Heath Park Tramway, Cardiff and the Collections Centre, Nantgarw are about 30 miles to the south east.

COLLECTIONS CENTRE, NANTGARW

Address

Collections Centre
Heol Crochendy
Parc Nantgarw
CF15 7QT

Tel: 029 2057 3560
Web: www.aocc.ac.uk
GR: ST140865
Gauge: 4' 8½"

Open

By prior appointment on weekdays, phone 029 2057 3560.

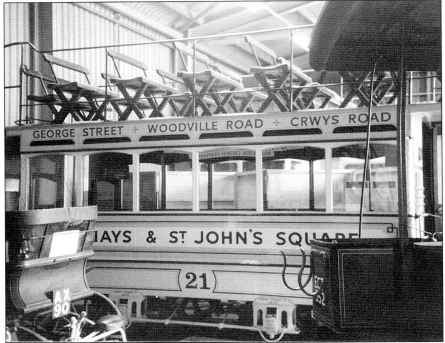

Cardiff horse tram 21 is at the Collections Centre, Nantgarw, this photograph was taken in its former location.

How to get there

Public transport: Travel by rail to Caerphilly Station. Walk away from the town centre, heading towards Nantgarw. The museum is about a mile down the road.
By car: From junction 32 of the M4 take the A470 north towards Merthyr Tydfil. At the second roundabout take the right exit to Nantgarw and Caerphilly. The museum is about a mile down that road.

Description

Following the closure of the Cardiff Industrial and Maritime Museum, the exhibits were transferred to the National Museums and Galleries of Wales Collections Centre located at Nantgarw, some eight miles north of Cardiff. The Centre is on the site of the former Nantgarw Colliery and is adjacent to the renowned nineteenth century Nantgarw pottery. The collection includes the preserved Cardiff horse tram. There is also an extensive reference library, archive and photographic archive relating to the industrial and transport history of Wales. Prior booking of all visits is essential.

Tram on display

System	No.	Built	Description
Cardiff	21	1886	4 wheel open top, unvestibuled, horse tram.

Nearby

The Heath Park Tramway, Cardiff is about 8 miles south and the Cefn Coed Colliery Museum, Crynant is about 30 miles to the north west.

CONWY VALLEY RAILWAY MUSEUM, BETWS Y COED

Address

Conwy Valley Railway Museum
Old Goods Yard
Betws-y-Coed
Aberconwy & Colwyn
LL24 0AL

Tel: 01690 710568
GR: SH792564
Gauge: 15"

A rare 15 inch gauge tramway can be found at Bets-y-coed in the Conwy Valley Railway Museum.

Open
Daily Easter to end October.

How to get there
By public transport: travel by train to Betws-y-Coed station. The museum is alongside the station.

By car: Betws-y-Coed is on the A5 by the junction with the Conwy Valley Road (A470) in the Snowdonia National Park. Travelling from Shrewsbury to Bangor the museum is on the right hand side in the centre of Betws-y-Coed. Ample free parking is available just beyond the museum site. Access is along the station platform and over the footbridge.

Description
Among the attractions at this railway museum, set in the North Wales town of Betws-y-Coed, is a working miniature tramway. Opened in 1991, the 15 inch gauge tramway carries passengers on a route alongside the full size railway at Betws-y-Coed station. The museum also has some of the superb Jack Nelson dioramas, one of which features a tram scene.

Tram on display

System	No.	Built	Description
Miniature tramcar	None	1991	Bogie, Cross Bench, vestibuled

Nearby
The Great Orme Tramway at Llandudno is about 18 miles north. Take the A470.

Liverpool streamline "Green Goddess" 869 resplendent at the Crich Tramway Village.

CRICH TRAMWAY VILLAGE (NATIONAL TRAMWAY MUSEUM)

Address

Crich Tramway Village
Home of the National Tramway Museum
Crich
Matlock
Derbyshire
DE4 5DP

Tel: 01773 852565
Web: www.tramway.co.uk
GR: SK345552
Gauge: 4' 8½"

Open

Weekends throughout the year and daily from 1 April to 31 October. Disabled access and tram riding.

How to get there

Public transport: Travel by rail to Whatstandwell Station Saturdays and Bank Holidays and then a long walk to the museum. Or go to Matlock or Belper stations and take a local bus to the museum. Bus times on "Busline" 01332 292200.

By car: The museum is set in the beautiful Derbyshire Peak District. It is immediately below the tower Memorial to the Sherwood Foresters, which is a helpful landmark when visiting the museum for the first time. From Junction 28 of the M1 take A38 west towards Derby. After about 7 miles the Tramway Museum is signposted on right (A610). After another 2 miles take signposted right under railway bridge, climbing steep hill. 1½ miles to Crich village. Take right at crossroads, up hill to junction, follow signs to left; this road leads to the free car park of the museum. From Derby take the A38 east towards the M1. After about 10 miles follow signs left to Tramway Museum (A610). Then as above.

Description

The Crich Tramway Village is the new name for the National Tramway Museum. It is recognised as the premier tramway museum in the world and is one of the few museums in Britain to be designated as having an outstanding national collection. It has over 50 tramcars from all parts of the British Isles and abroad. Tramcars are restored and maintained to the highest standards and there are always several tramcars giving tram rides on the two mile round trip. Many of the tramcars are displayed in the exhibition hall where a turn of the century tramway exhibition has been recreated. Visitors can walk around the depot buildings to see the other tramcars and special exhibits that are on display and there is a viewing gallery in the workshops.

The café and Red Lion pub provide hot and cold meals and drinks, or if preferred there is a large picnic area. Special events are held during the year, contact the museum for details. The museum shops sell souvenirs and a selection of tramway books.

Historians, researchers and students can use the extensive library and archives by appointment.

System	No.	Built	Description
Berlin	721039	1968	4 wheel single deck totally enclosed, in store.
Berlin	3006	1969	4 wheel, single deck, adapted for the disabled.
Blackpool	2	1928	4 wheel Railgrinder, in store.

System	No.	Built	Description
Blackpool	4	1884	4 wheel, open top, unvestibuled, conduit car.
Blackpool	5	1972	Bogie, single deck, totally enclosed.
Blackpool	40	1926	Bogie, balcony top, vestibuled, in store.
Blackpool	49	1926	Bogie, double deck totally enclosed.
Blackpool	59	1902	Bogie, open top, unvestibuled.
Blackpool	166	1927	Bogie, toastrack.
Blackpool	167	1928	Bogie, single deck, totally enclosed.
Blackpool	717	1927	4 wheel steeple cab locomotive.
Blackpool & Fleetwood	2	1898	Bogie, single deck, crossbench.
Brill	–	1906	4 wheel snow broom (ex Brussels 96).
Cardiff	131	1905	4 wheel water car, in store.
Chesterfield	7	1904	4 wheel, balcony top, unvestibuled.
Chesterfield	8	1899	Horse car, 4 wheel, single deck, enclosed
Crich	TW3	1979	Tower wagon.
Crich	--	1980	Crane wagon.
Den Haag	1147	1959	Bogie, single deck, totally enclosed.
Derby	1	1903	4 wheel, open top, unvestibuled.
Douglas Southern	1	1896	4 wheel, open top, unvestibuled.
Dundee	21	1894	Bogie, open top, steam trailer.
Edinburgh	35	1948	4 wheel, double deck totally enclosed.
Gateshead	5	1927	Bogie, single deck, totally enclosed.
Gateshead	52	1901	4 wheel, single deck, totally enclosed, in store.
Glasgow	22	1922	4 wheel, balcony top, vestibuled.
Glasgow	812	1900	4 wheel, double deck, totally enclosed.
Glasgow	1100	1928	Bogie, double deck, totally enclosed.
Glasgow	1115	1929	Bogie, double deck, totally enclosed.
Glasgow	1282	1940	Bogie, double deck, totally enclosed.

System	No.	Built	Description
Glasgow	1297	1948	Bogie, double deck, totally enclosed.
Glasgow	Works 1	1905	Cable car.
Glasgow	Works 12	1903	4 wheel welding car.
Grimsby & Immingham	14	1915	Bogie, single deck, totally enclosed.
Hill of Howth	10	1902	Bogie, open top, vestibuled.
Johannesburg	60	1905	4 wheel, balcony top, unvestibuled.
Leeds	180	1931	4 wheel, double deck, totally enclosed.
Leeds	345	1921	4 wheel, double deck, totally enclosed.
Leeds	399	1925	4 wheel, double deck, totally enclosed.
Leeds	600	1954	Bogie, single deck, totally enclosed.
Leeds	602	1953	Bogie, single deck, totally enclosed.
Leeds	TW 2	1932	Rail Derrick (Tower Wagon).
Leicester	76	1904	4 wheel, balcony top.
Liverpool	869	1936	Bogie, double deck, totally enclosed.
London County Council	106	1903	4 wheel, open top.
London Street Tramways	39	1870	Horse tram, one side only.
London Transport	1	1932	Bogie, double deck, totally enclosed.
London Transport	1622	1912	Bogie, double deck, totally enclosed.
Manchester	–	1911	Horse drawn tower wagon.
Manchester	W24	1879	Eades patent reversible truck (no body).
Metropolitan Electric Tys	331	1930	Bogie, double deck, totally enclosed.
New South Wales	47	1885	Steam tram locomotive.
Newcastle	102	1902	Bogie, open top, unvestibuled.
Oporto	9	1873	Horse car, 4 wheel, single deck.
Oporto	273	1927	Bogie, single deck, totally enclosed.
Paisley	68	1919	4 wheel, open top, unvestibuled.

System	No.	Built	Description
Prague	180	1908	4 wheel, single deck, totally enclosed.
Sheffield	15	1874	Horse car, 4 wheel, single deck, enclosed.
Sheffield	46	1899	4 wheel, single deck, totally enclosed.
Sheffield	74	1900	4 wheel, enclosed top, unvestibuled.
Sheffield	189	1934	4 wheel, double deck, totally enclosed.
Sheffield	264	1937	4 wheel, double deck, totally enclosed.
Sheffield	330	1920	4 wheel, single deck, totally enclosed.
Sheffield	510	1950	4 wheel, double deck, totally enclosed.
Sheffield	45	1903	4 wheel, open top, unvestibuled.
Southampton	–	1937	Tower wagon.
Third Avenue, New York	674	1939	Bogie, single deck, totally enclosed.
Warwick & Leamington	1	1881	Horse car, 4 wheel double deck.
?	?	?	Eades reversible horse car chassis, in store.

Nearby

Nottingham NET is around 15 miles south east and Sheffield Supertram is about 25 miles north.

CUMANN TRAENACH NA GAELTACHTA LAIR

Address

Cumann Traenach na Gaeltachta Lair
Fintown Station
Fintown
Co. Donegal
Ireland

Tel: 075 46280
Gauge: 3' 0"

It is unusual to find Charleroi trailers in Ireland, but there are three at Cumann Traenach na Gaeltachta Lair, Fintown.

Open
Daily June-September.

How to get there
By public transport: On my visit I saw no signs of any public transport. There should be a bus service between Letterkenny and Glenties which would stop at Fintown, but I cannot suggest how you get to either place.

By car: Fintown is on the R250 17 miles from Letterkenny and 9 miles from Glenties. Approaching from either direction the station is just off the road towards the lake. Fintown is a small community and the station is easy to find.

Description
One of the most famous of Ireland's 3ft gauge light railways is the County Donegal Railway. There are several movements to reopen parts of the line. This is the most advanced as a one mile section of track has been laid from the old Fintown Station towards Glenties. The motive power comes from an ex-mining diesel (they also have a Bord na Mona diesel locomotive). Of tramway interest is the passenger stock which consists of three ex-Charleroi (Belgium) tramway trailers. The first trip of the day is recommended as the superb views across Lough Finn to the mountains are supplemented by the entertainment of seeing the train crew drive the

sheep off the line. The tram trailers are considered to be second-hand running vehicles rather than preserved tramcars. They had a chequered history having been purchased by a private light railway in the Cotswolds, then going to Ulster to run on Shane's Castle Light Railway, where they were painted in the Shane's Castle livery. On moving to the Irish Republic two have been repainted in a red and cream livery representing the County Donegal colours.

Trams on display

System	No.	Built	Description
Charleroi	38	1915	4 wheel trailer, single deck, totally enclosed.
Charleroi	41	1915	4 wheel trailer, single deck, totally enclosed.
Charleroi	42	1915	4 wheel trailer, single deck, totally enclosed.

Nearby
There is nothing of tramway interest within easy travelling of Fintown.

DOVER TRANSPORT MUSEUM

Address
          The Dover Transport Museum
          Port Zone
          White Cliffs Business Park
          Dover
          CT16 2HT
Tel: 01304 822409
Web: www.dovertransportmuseum.co.uk
GR: TR305445
Gauge: 4' 8½"

Open
Sundays only. The new museum building is due to open soon.

How to get there
Public transport: Travel by train to Kearsney Station (just before Dover Priory).

Walk towards Dover to the roundabout. Take the left turn on to Whitfield Hill. After about a mile you will reach another roundabout; on the right is Gordon Road. Walk down Gordon Road to where it meets Menzies Road. Cross Menzies Road bearing right to Willingdon Road. The museum is about 100 yards down the road on the left.

By car: Leave the M2 at junction 7, the end of the motorway. Carry on the A2 by passing Canterbury towards Dover. On the approaches to Dover look for a round-about with a sign to Whitfield to the right. Take this road to the next roundabout, take the right turn on to Menzies Road. After 100 yards turn left into Willingdon Road. The museum is about 100 yards down the road on the left.

Description

The museum was formed in 1980 and is run by members of the Dover Transport Museum Society working as unpaid volunteers. The Society has preserved and restored many full size road vehicles, though not a Dover tramcar. The trams are represented by large scale working models operating on a layout. There is also the body of Maidstone demi-car number 18 that is in store awaiting restoration. This body was in the reserve store of the National Tramway Museum for many years, but unfortunately left in the open and has deteriorated badly. The tramcar needs totally rebuilding, which is a major task.

Tram in collection

System	No.	Built	Description
Maidstone	18	1909	4 wheel, single deck demi-car, in store awaiting restoration.

Nearby

The Folkestone Cliff Railway is just 9 miles down the coast

EAST ANGLIA TRANSPORT MUSEUM

Address

East Anglia Transport Museum
Chapel Road
Carlton Colville
Lowestoft
Suffolk NR33 8BL

Tel: 01502 518459
Fax: 01502 584658 www.eatm.org.uk
GR: TM505905
Gauge: 4' 8½"

Open

Easter week, Sundays and Bank Holidays May-September; Saturdays June-mid-July, every day mid July-August; Wednesdays and weekends September.

How to get there

Public transport: Travel by train to Lowestoft Station. In Waveney Road (opposite the station) catch bus L11 or L12 (Mondays to Saturdays) and alight at Carlton Colville Church or X71 or X74 (Mondays to Saturdays) and alight at Carlton Crown Public House. Walk up Chapel Road to the museum. On Sundays catch L18 or L19 which stop outside the museum.

By car: The museum is at Carlton Colville village, about 2 miles from Lowestoft. From Beccles take A146 approaching Lowestoft, turn right into Chapel Road (B1384) at Carlton Colville sign (just after the Crown Hotel). Down Chapel Road and museum is on right.

Description

The museum houses a large collection of road transport vehicles including the trams and trolleybuses. Rides on both trams and trolleybuses are given to the public. The tram route runs the length of the museum site and then curves into woodland. Usually both trams and trolleybuses are in operation. There is also a narrow gauge railway, souvenir shop and cafe. Visitors wanting meals and accommodation can obtain them at the Hedley House Hotel alongside the museum.

Trams on display

System	No.	Built	Description
Amsterdam	474	1929	4 wheel, single deck totally enclosed.
Blackpool	11	1939	Bogie, single deck, totally enclosed.
Blackpool	159	1929	Bogie, double deck, totally enclosed.
London Transport	1858	1930	Bogie, double deck, totally enclosed.
Lowestoft	14	1904	4 wheel, open top, unvestibuled.

Nearby
There is nothing of tramway interest within easy travelling distance.

You can ride on a London tramcar at the East Anglia Transport Museum.

GIANT'S CAUSEWAY AND BUSHMILLS RAILWAY

Address

Giant's Causeway Station
Runkerry Road
Bushmills
Co Antrim
BT57 8SZ

Tel: 028 2073 2594
Web: www.giantscausewayrailway.org
Gauge: 3' 0"

Open

Daily early May to end September.

How to get there

Public transport: Probably the best way to get to the railway would be to join a coach trip to the Giant's Causeway. The railway is a few minutes walk from the visitors centre.

By car: The best approach to the Giant's Causeway is from the former station at Portrush, where the tramway started. Portrush is on the A29 from Coleraine. The former station is in the centre of town and the building still looks very much the same as it did in the days of the tram. From the station building drive north to the first junction, Methodist Corner. Here turn very sharp right (following the track of the tramway) into Causeway Street and drive out of Portrush. On the outskirts of the town look for a filling station and garage on the left. These are the former tram depot buildings. Following the road along the coast proceed towards Bushmills. Parts of the track bed of the tramway can be identified on the left side (seaward side) of the road as a raised footpath, particularly at the passing places. On the approaches to Bushmills the former Bushmills station can be seen; it is now a private house. Opposite the station building is the start of the railway with a small car park. Alternatively drive into Bushmills and turn left at the crossroads following the signs to the Giant's Causeway. The Giant's Causeway station is well signposted and has plenty of parking.

Description

I am unsure if this is a valid entry for this guide. The original entry referred to the replica tramcar in the Visitors Centre. However following the fire that destroyed the buildings the tram was broken up and scrapped. The new centre makes no obvious reference to the tramway. However, a new steam railway has been constructed on the track bed of the old tramway. A two-mile section is used, from the Causeway to Bushmills. Apart from the natural attraction of the Giant's Causeway itself, the railway is of interest because it allows rail travel on the route of the first electric tramway in the British Isles. Also there are plans to erect overhead and build replicas of the original tramcars to run on the line. Phone or check the web site for the latest situation.

Nearby

The Ulster Folk and Transport Museum is about 50 miles to the east. But while here a visit to the Causeway and a tour of the famous Bushmills whisky distillery are essential.

GLASGOW MUSEUM OF TRANSPORT

Address

Glasgow Museum of Transport
Kelvin Hall
1 Bunhouse Road
Glasgow
G3 8DP

Tel: 0141 287 2720
GR: NS555667
Gauge: 4' 8½"

Open

All year except Christmas Day, Boxing Day and 1st and 2nd January.

How to get there

By public transport: The easiest way is by underground. Leaving Kelvin Hall Station walk down Argyle Street towards the city centre. The Museum is in Bunhouse Road on the right.

By car: Park at one of the park and ride Underground stations, Shields Road, West Street and Bridge Street stations south of the Clyde and Kelvinbridge station north of the river. Then travel to Kelvin Hall Station and follow the above directions.

Description

The famous Kelvin Hall has been developed into a magnificent transport museum. The only attraction that it lacks is an operating tramway. All the tram exhibits (indeed all exhibits) are static. In addition to the trams there are displays of the Glasgow Underground (with a reconstructed station), trolleybuses, steam locomotives, cars, commercial vehicles, bicycles and ship models. Well worth allowing

There is a fine selection of tramcars at the Glasgow Museum of Transport.

plenty of time to see the whole museum. Hot and cold meals are available from the catering area and there is a souvenir shop.

Trams on display

System	No.	Built	Description
Glasgow	543	1894	Horse car, 4 wheel, open top.
Glasgow	672	1898	Bogie, single deck, unvestibuled.
Glasgow	779	1900	4 Wheel, balcony top, unvestibuled.
Glasgow	1088	1924	4 Wheel, double deck, totally enclosed.
Glasgow	1089	1926	Bogie, single deck, totally enclosed.
Glasgow	1173	1938	Bogie, double deck, totally enclosed.
Glasgow	1392	1952	Bogie, double deck, totally enclosed.
Glasgow	39T	1898	Bogie, single deck short trailer car, Underground Railway
Glasgow	?	1898	Bogie rebuilt long power car, Underground Railway

Nearby

Glasgow Underground and Coatbridge Summerlee Heritage Park.

GLYN VALLEY TRAMWAY

Address

Glyn Valley Tramway
Glyn Ceiriog
Nr Llangollen

Tel: 01691 718218
GR: SJ205380
Gauge: 2' 4½"

Open

Monday-Friday April-October, closed weekends and Bank Holidays.

How to get there

Public transport: Travel by train to Chirk Station which is about six miles away from Glyn Ceiriog, on the B4500. A long walk, but for most of the way you will be following the route of the tramway.

By car: At the third roundabout on the A5 north of Oswestry take the second left road towards Chirk. In Chirk take the B4500 to Pontfadog and Glyn Ceirog. After about four miles drive through Pontfadog and a mile further on is Glyn Ceiriog.

Description

The Glyn Valley Tramway Group have established two areas of interest. A small museum about the tramway has been developed in the Glyn Valley Hotel, which is open during licensing hours. A mile down the road at Pontfadog they have restored the former tramway waiting room. It is open to the public Monday-Friday from April to October (note it is closed weekends and Bank Holidays). If closed ask for the key at the chapel next door. A Glyn Valley coach is preserved on the Talyllyn railway.

Nearby

The Conwy Valley Railway Museum is about 25 miles north on the A5.

GRAMPIAN TRANSPORT MUSEUM

Address

Grampian Transport Museum
Alford
Aberdeenshire
Tel: 019755 62292
GR: NJ580164
Gauge: 3' 6"

Open

Daily April to September.

How to get there

By public transport: the nearest railway station is at Aberdeen, some 25 miles away. Outside the station is the bus station. Here take a Bluebird coach to Alford. Ask for the nearest bus stop in Alford to the Grampian Museum.
By car: Alford is approximately 25 miles west of Aberdeen on the A944. The Grampian Transport Museum is signposted on the A944, with car parking.

Description

The museum houses a general transport collection with vintage and classic cars, trains, buses, bikes, motor bikes and two trams. Restored to original condition is Aberdeen horse tram number 1 and a Cruden Bay tramcar. This 3 ft 6 in gauge tramway was built by the Great North of Scotland Railway to connect their main line railway with the Cruden Bay Hotel. There were two tramcars and the best parts of each have been used to reconstruct this tramcar. The museum has a souvenir shop.

While in Alford visit the Alford Valley Railway to see the Aberdeen Suburban tramcar (see separate entry).

Trams on display

System	No.	Built	Description
Aberdeen	1	1896	4 wheel, horse tram.
Cruden Bay	1/2	1899	4 wheel single deck, unvestibuled, large platform

Nearby

The Alford Valley Railway is also in Alford.

GREAT CENTRAL RAILWAY

Address

Great Central Station
Quorndon
Loughborough
Leicestershire LE11 1RW

Tel: 01509 230726
GR: SK549158
Web: www.gcrailway.co.uk
Gauge: 1 metre

Open

Daily late May to August, Weekends and Bank Holidays all year.

How to get there

By public transport: travel by rail to Loughborough Midland station. There is no bus service to the Great Central preserved line. It is a 15 minute brisk walk. Walk from the station to the traffic lights. Go straight across (as if going into the town centre) and continue over a canal bridge to a second set of traffic lights. At these lights take the first left and after half a mile the road veers to the right. The station should be in sight on the left. You will then need to ride on the preserved railway to Quorndon station where the tram is stored.

By car: The tram is at Quorndon and the grid reference and direction are given for Quorndon station and not the main station at Loughborough. From junction 23 of the M1 take the A512 towards Loughborough. At the roundabout with the ring road take the right hand exit, following signs to Great Central Railway. Follow ring road to its junction with the A6. Turn south towards Leicester. At the next roundabout take second exit towards Quorndon (well signposted for Great Central Railway). After a few hundred yards turn right at traffic lights. The Great Central railway Station is signposted on the left about half a mile from the traffic lights. There is a large car park.

Description

The Great Central Railway is a preserved steam railway. They gave storage space to the two Krefeld (Germany) tramcars that were presented to Leicester (Leicester is twinned with Krefeld). Plans to open a working tramway in Abbey Park fell through and storage of the trams became difficult and the Great Central Railway agreed to give them space. The power bogie car has been moved to storage in Walthamstow, while the trailer is still gently rotting at Quorndon Station.

As the tramcar is metre gauge it will not run on the standard gauge railway line.

Trams on display

System	No.	Built	Description
Krefeld	41	1956	4 wheel, Trailer, single deck, totally enclosed.

Nearby

Nottingham NET is about 15 miles north and Crich Tramway Village about 25 miles north west.

HEATH PARK TRAMWAY, CARDIFF

Address

Heath Park Miniature Railway and Tramway
Heath Park
King George Vth Drive East
Heath
Cardiff
GR: ST176800
Web: www.cardiffmes.com
Gauge: 18"

Open

Public running days are on limited weekends, see events section of Railway Modeller for dates.

How to get there

By public transport: Travel by rail to Heath Low Level station or to Heath High Level station, both being within easy walking distance of the park.

By car: From Junction 29 of the M4 take the A48M towards Cardiff. This turns into the A48, stay on for seven junctions. At the A470/A469 junction leave the A48. Take the A469 towards Caerphilly. At traffic lights just before a railway bridge turn right into Heath Park Avenue. Drive past traffic calming measures and take the first right, King George V Drive. At the roundabout at the end of this short road turn left. The park is on the right, look for a narrow road into the park, it is the first on the right. Take this to a car park next to the miniature railway.

Description

The Whitchurch (Cardiff) Model Engineering Society has its running tracks in Heath Park. Mostly railway (with 3½", 5" and 7¼" steam railways) there is a passenger-carrying 18" gauge electric tramway approximately 250 yards long. The two tramcars were designed by the late Felix Cunuder, formerly Chief Engineer to Cardiff Corporation Transport, and built by Society members.

Trams on display

System	No.	Built	Description
Heath Park	1	1973	4 wheel, single deck, crossbench, unvestibuled.
Heath Park	2	1976	Bogie, single deck, California car.

Nearby

The Collections Centre, Nantgarw is about 8 miles to the north and the Cefn Coed Colliery Museum, Crynant is about 30 miles to the north west.

HEATON PARK VINTAGE TRAMWAY, MANCHESTER

Address

Heaton Park Vintage Tramway
Middleton Road
Manchester

Tel: 0161 740 1919 or 01204 528922
GR: SD830042
Gauge: 4' 8½"

Open

Afternoons Sundays and Bank Holidays Good Friday to second Sunday in October: Wednesdays June and July.

How to get there

By public transport: There is only one way for the tram enthusiast to get to the Heaton Park tramway and that is by the Manchester Metro. Alight from Bowker Vale station (on the Bury line). Turn left out of the station and walk along

The Heaton Park Vintage Tramway gives a very enjoyable ride in the park.

Middleton Road. A short distance along the road you will see elaborate Park Gates behind which is the terminus of the tram route. If there is no tram in sight the overhead wires will show you are in the right place. Enter the park and walk alongside the tram track to the building you can see a hundred yards away. This is the depot and museum and the boarding place for a tram ride.

Description

This operating standard gauge tramway gives the opportunity to ride in the most attractive setting of the tree lined park roads. The total run is about a mile for the return trip. About half way along is the small depot. This is open with a sales counter and small display. There is little better than riding on the Manchester combination car on a warm summer's day to the lakeside. In the depot is a small museum containing the history and a collection of items from the Manchester tramway days. There is also an operating 1:16 scale model tramway.

Trams on display

System	No.	Built	Description
Hull	96	1901	4 wheel, single deck, totally enclosed.
Manchester Carriage & Tramways Co.	L53	1879	4 wheel, horse tram, open top.
Manchester	765	1914	Bogie, single deck, combination.

Nearby
The Manchester Metrolink is a short walk away. Ride it to the Manchester Museum of Transport.

LAUNCESTON STEAM RAILWAY

Address
Launceston Steam Railway
St Thomas Road
Launceston
Cornwall PL5 8DA
Tel: 01566 775665
GR: SX330851
Gauge: 1' 11½"

Open
Daily except Saturdays July to end September. For opening days outside these months contact the railway.

How to get there
By public transport: In researching the last edition I was told by the railway that getting to them by public transport was not easy. This situation has not improved. Travel by rail to Plymouth Station and there is a bus connection to Launceston. In addition, on Sundays only, there is a rover ticket and a service from Exeter to Launceston Railway. Phone the bus company for details on 01392 382800.
By car: Launceston is just north of the A30, the main road from Exeter into Cornwall. Turn off the A30 to the town centre. Take the B3254 north towards Bude. The Steam Railway is just up the road, not far from the town centre, car parking is available.

Description

This is really a 1' 11½" gauge steam railway museum. It uses mainly ex-quarry locomotives. The tramway interest comes from two crossbench passenger carriages that have been built to a design based on Manx Electric trailer cars and a four wheel saloon tramcar similar to horse drawn trams. There is also a museum of vintage cars and motorcycles. There is a cafe and gift shop for visitors. Launceston is also the home of the former North Bay funicular from Scarborough, which closed in 1996. It was donated to the Launceston Civic Society by Scarborough Borough Council. The proposal was to erect it as a link between an industrial estate built on the site of the former railway stations and the town. So far no firm moves have been made and the funicular remains in a dismantled condition in store in Launceston.

Trams on display

System	No.	Built	Description
Manx Electric	1	1981	Modelled on Manx Electric bogie crossbench trailer.
Manx Electric	2	1988	Modelled on Manx Electric bogie crossbench trailer.
	67	1983	Similar to four wheel horse tramcar

Nearby

The nearest other tramway interest is the Babbacombe cliff railway at Torquay, some 40 miles to the east.

LISTOWEL AND BALLYBUNION MONORAIL

One of the most unusual forms of public railed transport has to be the "Lartigue" or Listowel and Ballybunion Monorail. The market town of Listowel joined the main line railway in 1880 when the Great Southern and Western Railway opened their line from Limerick to Tralee. The coastal town of Ballybunion felt that if they could get a rail link to the main line at Listowel they would be able to sell sand to the building industry and also develop Ballybunion as a tourist resort. The first proposal was for a three-foot gauge tramway, but this fell through as did an idea to build a standard gauge (5' 3") line. Both were too costly.

Then Charles Francois Marie-Therese Lartigue, a Spanish inventor living in Paris, patented a unique monorail, where the carriages and locomotives were slung pannier style over an 'A' framework of rails. He offered to build the rail connection, using his new system, for £33,000, which included the purchase of the necessary land. It was agreed and the line was built in a remarkably short time of five months. It formally opened on 29 February 1888. It operated until October 1924 when, owing to operating losses, it closed. However, interest in this very unusual transport continued with many articles and books being written about it. There are two particular places of interest for anyone who wants to see more about the line.

LISTOWEL AND BALLYBUNION – 1

PRESERVED MONORAIL, LISSELTON

Address
        Michael Barry
        Ballingowan Farm
        Lisselton
        Kerry
Gauge: Monorail

Open
Visible from the roadside.

A short section of the unique Listowel and Ballybunion monorail has been found and restored by Michael Barry at his farm in Lisselton.

How to get there

Public transport: The nearest railway station is Tralee, some 15 miles from Listowel. A bus connection will take you to Listowel and another bus to Lisselton. But the bad news is that it is still a long walk to the farm – about three to four miles. Follow the instructions set out below from the crossroads at Lisselton.

By car: Listowel is on the N69 between Tralee and Limerick. From Listowel take the R553 towards Ballybunion. Five miles from Listowel is the community of Lisselton. It is easily identified as it is the only crossroads and there is a pub, garage and a shop. At these crossroads turn right, but slowly, because you will need to turn left immediately after the shop. Follow this narrow road, taking the first left (about a mile to two from the shop). After a short distance take the first left along a very narrow road, there is a sign pointing to "Barrys". Follow this road to the end, about half a mile. At the end is the farm and just before the farm you will see the section of restored track and a carriage.

Description

For over forty years Michael Barry has been fascinated by the monorail and has made it his mission to collect every part of the original line he can. Given that the line was sold for scrap in 1924 and taken away, it is amazing that any has survived. In fact Michael Barry has found sufficient to reconstruct a short length of line and one carriage, number 1. These are on display next to his farm house. If you are lucky, as I was, Mr Barry will be there and tell you about the line and how he has gathered the parts and built the section of line.

Nearby

The replica monorail in Listowel.

LISTOWEL AND BALLYBUNION – 2

REPLICA MONORAIL, LISTOWEL

Address

The Lartigue Monorail
Listowel
Lisselton
Kerry
Tel: 068 24393
Web: www.homepage.eircom.net/~lartiguemonorail
Gauge: Monorail

Open

Daily April to September, afternoons only. Trains run every hour on the hour.

How to get there

Follow the directions set out for the previous entry as far as Listowel. From the town square the monorail is north. Follow the signs for the R552 into Lower William Street. Walk along this road and turn left into Market Street, signposted to Ballybunion, R553. Market Street becomes Convent Street. Take the second right, again signposted to Ballybunion, R553. Then take the second right, the Lartigue is on the corner, over the road.

Description

For over three years Listowel has been gathering finance for a major project to attract tourists to the town. It has recreated a section of the Lartigue Monorail. A replica locomotive and carriages have been built by Alan Keefe. The locomotive has the outline of the original steam locomotive, but is driven by a small diesel engine. I saw the line in April, a month before it opened and everything was shut away out of sight, only the track being visible. What I saw looked superb and absolutely fascinating.

Nearby

The preserved section of monorail in Lisselton.

In Listowel a section of the monorail has been recreated as a tourist attraction. Unfortunately I visited it before it was open, so could only photograph the track.

The Lechwedd Stale Caverns has a steep funicular to take visitors underground to the deep caverns.

LLECHWEDD SLATE CAVERNS – BLAENAU FFESTINIOG

Address
Llechwedd Slate
Caverns
Blaenau Ffestiniog
Gwynedd
LL41 3NB
Tel: 01766 830306
E-mail: llechwedd@aol.com
Web: www.llechwedd.co.uk
GR: SH699470
Gauge: 3' 0"

Open
All year (closed 25th-26th December and 1st January)

How to get there
By public transport: travel by rail to Blaenau Ffestiniog station (either by standard

gauge on the Llandudno Junction line, or narrow gauge on the Ffestiniog Railway). There are bus links to Llechwedd from the station.

By car: Blaenau Ffestiniog is on the A470 between Dolgellau and Betwys-y-Coed. Llechwedd Slate Caverns are situated on the north side of the town with the entrance on the A470. There is plenty of parking on site.

Description

Llechwedd Slate Caverns offer two underground rides to the visitor. Each requires payment of an entrance fee. The first is the Deep Mine. Here the tour starts with a ride down on a steep funicular, claimed to be the steepest passenger railway in Britain at 1 in 1.8. However, no indication is given as to how this is calculated, and the railway is noticeably less steep in the lower portion, so it is not possible to verify this claim, particularly as the East Hill Cliff at Hastings is 1 in 1.28. A single carriage runs on a 420ft long 3' gauge line through a tunnel with little room to spare. The carriage is stepped, with small compartments with just enough space for six people. The ride takes the visitors down to the lower portion of the caverns. Here they disembark and have a 25 minute walk with 10 son et lumière tableaux, which includes descending a level. The return is by the funicular, this time at a lower station. The funicular is powered by an electric motor and there is no counter balance. So it operates like a lift, all the weight being taken by the motor and winding gear. The second ride is by the Miner's Tramway. A 450 yard long, 2' gauge light railway with small cross bench carriages hauled by a small mine locomotive takes visitors on a level track into the upper caverns of the slate quarry.

Tickets

There is a charge for each tour which includes the ride.

Nearby

The Conwy Railway Museum at Betws-y-Coed is about 10 miles north and the cliff railway at Machynlleth, Centre for Alternative Technology is about 30 miles south.

LONDON TRANSPORT MUSEUM

Address

London Transport Museum
Covent Garden Piazza
London WC2E 7BB

Tel: 020 7565 7299 (24 hour recording) or 020 7379 6344

GR: TQ310824
Gauge: 4' 8½"

Open

All year except 24, 25, 26 December

How to get there

Public transport: Go on the Piccadilly Underground Line to Covent Garden Station. Coming out of the station turn right and head for the old Covent Garden market. When facing the market area you will find the museum in the far left corner, but it is not visible until you get on to the cobbled area to the north of Covent Garden.

By car: Travel by car cannot be recommended. Park by an Underground station on the outer parts of the system. Then go to Covent Garden station as above.

Description

Another museum where the tram exhibits are static. The museum has tried to overcome this by a number of inventive 'hands on' exhibits, though not incorporating the trams. However, you can get on the E/1 and handle the controls. In addition to the full size exhibits there are many superb tram models, including a working large scale model of the Docklands Light Railway. There is a large sales shop and cafe, both accessible without paying to go into the museum.

Trams on display

System	No.	Built	Description
London Tramways Co.	284	1881	Horse car, 4 wheel, open top.
London Transport	1025	1908	Bogie, double deck, totally enclosed.
MET	355	1931	Bogie, double deck, totally enclosed.
West Ham	102	1910	4 wheel, balcony top, unvestibuled.

Nearby

Docklands Light Railway, Croydon Tramlink, London funicular.

LYNNE TAIT GALLERY, OLD LEIGH

Address

Lynne Tait Gallery
The Old Foundry
High Street
Old Leigh
Essex
GR: TQ830855
Gauge: 3' 6"

Open

The gallery is open all year.

How to get there

Public transport: Travel by rail to Leigh-on-Sea Station. On leaving the station turn right and then take the lower of the two roads facing you, Belton Gardens, and walk above and alongside the railway line. Take the first right, Belton Bridge, and at the bottom of the ramp go straight across the roundabout into the High Street. The gallery is about 200 yards on the left.

By car: From junction 30 of the M25 take the A13 towards Southend. After about

The Centre for Alternative Technology turned to the water balance principle when they built a new funicular to take visitors from the car park to the upper levels of the Centre at Machynlleth.

20 miles look for signposts to Leigh, and turn off the A13 towards Leigh looking for signs to Leigh-on-Sea station. Past Leigh station take the lower of the two roads facing you, Belton Gardens, and drive above and alongside the railway line. Take the first right, Belton Bridge, and at the bottom of the ramp go straight across the roundabout into the High Street. Drive about 200 yards. The gallery is on the left with a small adjoining pay and display car park. Parking is very limited, but there is some more pay and display on the railway side of the ramp off the bridge. Go back along the High Street and at the roundabout turn right and you will see the parking.

Description

This was a surprise to me. Usually I get told about trams and I make a dedicated trip to see them. This time I was in Southend visiting the family. We were taken to Old Leigh and in the Lynne Tait Gallery, a card and gift shop, there was a complete carriage from the old Southend Pier Railway. It was used as a store and support for displaying items for sale.

Tram on display

System	No.	Built	Description
Southend Pier	21	1949	4 wheel, single deck, totally enclosed.

Nearby

Southend funicular and Southend Pier Railway and Museum.

MACHYNLLETH, CENTRE FOR ALTERNATIVE TECHNOLOGY CLIFF RAILWAY

Address

Centre for Alternative Technology
Machynlleth
Powys
SY20 9AZ

Tel: 01654 702400
Web: www.cat.org.uk
GR: SH754044
Gauge: 1·6 metres

Open

The Centre is open all year, but the cliff railway only operates from Easter to October inclusive.

How to get there

By public transport: travel by rail to Machynlleth station. From here take a connecting bus (Arriva Cymru route 32) to the Centre, the nearest bus stop to the Centre is 300 metres away. All Wales transport information 0870 608 2608.

By car: there is no close motorway, so make your way to Machynlleth. From there take the A487 towards Dolgellau. The Centre is on the right, less than 3 miles along the road. It is well signposted and there is a free car park at the entrance to the Centre.

Description

The Centre for Alternative Technology (CAT) was set up to show how we can live in harmony with the environment without destroying our life support systems. In 1992 a water balance cliff railway was opened to save visitors walking up a steep path from the entrance and at the same time to demonstrate passenger travel using the minimum of external power. The twin 5' 3" gauge tracks give a ride of 175ft, with the upper station about 100ft above the lower one. Being the most modern water balance cliff railway in the country, modern technology has been used. So the weights of the cars and the passengers are compared by a computer, which then allows the appropriate amount of water into the upper car to operate the railway. After the journey the water in the lower car is released to a reservoir and pumped back to the top lake. The water in the lake goes through a turbine before being used by the railway. This provides power for the return pump. It is claimed that the railway uses just 20 watts of fuel (much less than the average house light bulb.) The carriages are named "Annie" and "Martha".

Tickets

Free travel on the cliff railway, after paying the entrance fee to the centre.

Nearby

The cliff railway at Aberystwyth is about 20 miles south and the cliff railway at the Llechwed Slate Caverns is about 30 miles north.

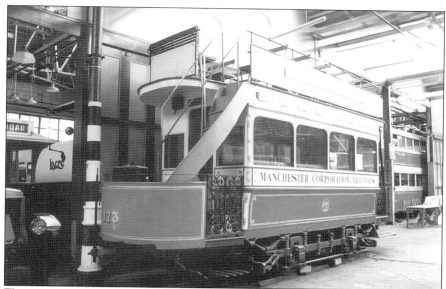

The restored Manchester tramcar 173 at Manchester Museum of Transport. It is hoped the tramcar will be able to run on the Heaton Park Vintage Tramway.

MANCHESTER MUSEUM OF TRANSPORT

Address

Manchester Museum of Transport
Boyle Street
Cheetham Hill
Manchester
M8 8UW

Tel: 0161 205 2122
Web: www.gmpte.gov.uk
GR: SD846007
Gauge: 4' 8½"

Open

All year every Wednesday, Saturday, Sunday and all Bank Holidays except Christmas Day and Boxing day.

How to get there

By public transport: take the Metrolink to Woodlands Road stop. From there turn right and walk along Woodlands Road, continue on to Smedley Road. At the end of Smedley Road is Queens Road. Turn right and walk along until you reach Boyle Street on your right. Proceed along Boyle Street alongside the bus garage until you reach the museum.

By car: The museum is 1¼ miles north from Manchester city centre. By car from the city centre follow the signs to Bury A665. The museum is signposted on the right when leaving the city. At the traffic lights turn right into Queens Road. Take the first left into Boyle Street. Drive past the bus depot, the entrance to the museum is at the far end. Limited free parking available.

Description

This is mainly a bus museum with other aspects of public transport including trams. There is a nice selection of small scale tramcar models and a variety of smaller tramway related items are displayed, including a tramcar GPO letter box used in Manchester. The museum includes a tea room and souvenir shop.

Trams on display or in collection

System	No.	Built	Description
Manchester	173	1901	4 wheel, open top, unvestibuled.
Manchester Metrolink	1000	1990	Pre-production mock up, "The Larry Sullivan".
South Lancashire	65	1906	4 wheel, open top, waiting restoration

Nearby

The Manchester Metrolink is a short walk away, ride it to Heaton Park Vintage Tramway or the funicular at the Urbis Museum.

MANX TRANSPORT MUSEUM

Address

The Brickworks Office
Mill Road
Peel
Isle of Man

Tel: 01624 842448 or 01624 827855
GR: SC243840
Gauge: 3' 0"

The history of Cunningham's Camp Escalator can be found in the Manx Transport Museum, but you will need to go to Douglas to see the remains of the lower entrance.

Open

Saturdays, Sundays and Bank Holidays Easter to the end of September. Also Tuesday and Thursday in TT Race Week. Private parties outside normal opening hours welcome by prior arrangement.

How to get there

Public transport: There are two ways to get to the Isle of Man. By air to Ronaldsway Airport or by ferry landing at Douglas. From Douglas, Lord Street Bus Station, between the sea terminal and the railway station, bus routes 5, 5A, 6 6A and X5 go to Peel.

By car: If you have taken your car across on the ferry, or hired a car on the island, take the A1 from Douglas to Peel. In Peel drive down to the shore and turn left. Drive along into Victoria Road and then you will have to turn sharp left alongside the river on East Quay. Pass by the House of Manannan Museum, on your left, to where Mill Road joins East Quay. Turn sharp left into Mill Road. The Transport Museum is immediately on the right, with a large car park next to it.

Description

The Manx Transport Group, formed in 1993, has leased the former Peel Brickworks Office building and has restored it. It is now a small transport museum devoted to all forms of transport on the Isle of Man. At first glance it would not appear to have room for anything of interest with just two small rooms in the building. But in the first room look under the table in the centre of the room. This in fact is the luggage trailer from the Queens Pier tramway in Ramsey. The exhibit includes a small section of pier decking with the rails in it. Also in the room is a model and information on Cunningham's Camp Escalator. This most unusual type of funicular was built in Douglas to serve a tented holiday camp site above the town. It opened in 1923 and closed in 1967. The escalator itself still exists, though abandoned and in a sorry state. To see it go to Douglas promenade. Go along the promenade to the Hydro Hotel. Walk into Switzerland Road.

The road bends sharply right, and immediately ahead is the façade of the entrance to the escalator. To the left of the façade the roof over the escalator can just be made out amongst the trees and undergrowth.

Trams on display

System	No.	Built	Description
Queens Pier Ramsey	–	1886	Luggage trailer.

Nearby

In Douglas there is the Douglas Horse Tramway which connects with the Manx Electric Railway and meets the Snaefell Mountain Railway at Laxey. Also in Douglas is the Manx Museum.

MILESTONES MUSEUM, BASINGSTOKE

Address

	Milestones Museum
	Leisure Park
	Churchill Way
	Basingstoke
	Hampshire
Tel:	01256 477766
GR:	SU625525
Gauge:	4' 7¾"

A new museum has opened in Basingstoke with a restored Portsmouth tramcar.

Open

Closed Mondays except Bank Holidays, open all year except Christmas Day, Boxing Day and New Years Day.

How to get there

Public transport: Travel by rail to Basingstoke Station. The museum is two miles from the station. There is a shuttle bus every 8-10 minutes during day time between the station and the leisure park with a stop outside the museum. For details ring 07753 719381.

By car: From junction 6 of the M3 drive to the first roundabout, take the left exit on to the ring road. Stay on the ring road to the "Thorneycroft Roundabout" and take the left exit on to the B3400 signposted to Whitchurch/Andover. The leisure park is on the right. Enter through entrance "B" and turn right. The museum is directly ahead with car parking.

Description

The museum creates an open air museum but under cover. A network of streets and buildings has been built to represent typical streets in Hampshire from the Victorian times to the 1930s. Included in one of the street scenes is a restored

Portsmouth tramcar. The tram has its own interest as it is the only surviving example of a horse tram that was converted for electrical operation when the council took over the tramway system.

Tram on display

System	No.	Built	Description
Portsmouth	84	1880	4 wheel, open top horse tram converted to electric operation in 1902.

Nearby
The Hythe Pier tramway is about 35 miles south west.

MILTON KEYNES MUSEUM

Address
      Milton Keynes Museum
      Off McConnell Drive
      Southern Way
      Wolverton
      MK12 5EJ
Tel: 01908 316222
Web: www.artizan.co.uk/mkm
GR: SP822407
Gauge: 3' 6"

Open
April – October, Wednesdays to Sundays (inclusive) and Bank Holiday Mondays.

How to get there
By public transport: travel by rail to Milton Keynes station. Outside the station take a number 6 or 6A bus that goes direct to Stacey Hall, where the museum is situated.

By car: Since the last edition things have improved a bit for me in Milton Keynes. I can now get to the museum without getting lost. From Junction 14 of the M1 take the A509 towards Milton Keynes. Stay on the A509 until you reach the A5. Take the A5 north to the next junction (A422). Do not take the A422, take the road

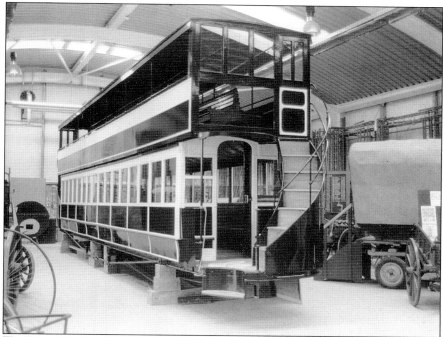

The Wolverton and Stony Stratford Tramway ran near what is now Milton Keynes. The museum there has restored one of the massive steam tram trailers.

immediately before it. At the next roundabout turn right into Millers Way. The museum is signposted on the left, turn left into McConnell Drive to get to the entrance.

If you accidentally find yourself on the A422 do not worry, carry on straight over the first roundabout then left at the second roundabout. This is Millers· Way, the museum is about half a mile on the right. Take the right turn into McConnell Drive. There is plenty of parking space at the Museum.

Description

The museum aims to show how the lives of ordinary people have changed over the past two hundred years.

Part of the display is a Transport Hall which contains a steam tram trailer from the Wolverton and Stony Stratford Tramway. These trailers were some of the largest tramcars built, seating 100 passengers. The restoration of number 2 is almost complete and it dominates all the other exhibits in the hall. The upper deck of number 5 in an unrestored state and the remains of the lower deck are also at the Museum, but not on public display. It may be viewed by prior arrangement with the museum. A diorama with a model of the steam locomotive and two trailers forms part of the tramway exhibit.

The rest of the museum is well worth a look and the volunteers working at the museum are very helpful. There is also a special display covering the history of telephones. There is a coffee shop and souvenir shop.

Trams on display or in collection

System	No.	Built	Description
Wolverton & S Stratford	2	1887	Bogie, double deck trailer under restoration.
Wolverton & S Stratford	5	1888	Bogie, double deck trailer upper deck only, in store.

Nearby

Stockwood Craft Museum in Luton, with the superb model trams, is about 15 miles south east.

MUSEUM OF ELECTRICITY, CHRISTCHURCH, BOURNEMOUTH

Address

The Museum of Electricity
The Old Power Station
Bargates
Christchurch
Dorset
BH23 1QE

Tel: 01202 480467
GR: SZ155933
Gauge: 3' 6"

Open

Mondays to Fridays only, Easter to September inclusive

How to get there

By public transport: travel by rail to Christchurch station. Leave station and walk to Bargates, turn right and walk along shops. Stop at Castles the ironmongers (very

Bournemouth 85 is on display at the Museum of Electricity in Christchurch, Dorset.

distinctive with a bright yellow shop front), look right, and you will see the museum entrance opposite. Cross road and walk down driveway to the old power station.

By car: from the end (junction 1) of the M27 take the A337 to Lyndhurst. At Lyndhurst take the A35 to Christchurch. In the centre of Christchurch you will encounter a strange double roundabout with the town centre indicated to the left at the second of the two roundabouts. Do not take this, but continue round the round-about and turn into Bargates. Drive slowly up Bargates looking for Castles the ironmongers on the left (with a bright yellow frontage). At Castles turn immediately right into a driveway which leads to the Old Power Station.

Description

This small museum has been set up by Scottish and Southern Energy plc. It has an interesting collection of items associated with the history of electrical supply. Most seem to be domestic appliances, but of interest to us is the restored Bournemouth tramcar number 85. The power station is an appropriate home not only because of the electrical connection but also because Bournemouth trams used to run along Bargates.

Tram on display

System	No.	Built	Description
Bournemouth	85	1914	Bogie, double deck, open top, became Llandudno No 6.

Nearby
The Bournemouth cliff railways are about five miles west along the coast.

NATIONAL COAL MINING MUSEUM FOR ENGLAND, CAPHOUSE COLLIERY

Address
National Coal Mining Museum for England
Caphouse Colliery
New Road
Overton
Wakefield
Yorkshire WF4 4RH
Tel: 01924 848806
GR: SE253168
Gauge: 2' 3"

Open
All year (except 24-25th December and 1st January)

How to get there
By public transport: travel by rail to either Huddersfield or Wakefield Westgate stations. Take the bus link between the two towns. The museum is about halfway between Huddersfield and Wakefield with bus stops within easy walking distance. *By car:* from junction 24 of the M62 follow the signs to Huddersfield. Drive towards the town centre until you reach the ring road. Follow the signs for A642 Wakefield. The museum is about 6 miles from Huddersfield on the A642 on the left and is well signposted. There is parking on site.

Description
Caphouse Colliery ceased to be an active mine in 1989. It was opened up as the Yorkshire Mining Museum and is now known as the National Coal Mining

The National Coal Mining Museum near Wakefield has a cable hauled tramway that demonstrates the type of transport used to carry miners to the coalface. These are two typical carriages on static display.

Museum of England. The main attraction is an hour-long tour of the mine starting with a drop of 450ft in the mine cage. On the surface the museum has a most unusual form of cable hauled passenger tramway. Called a "Paddy Train" the museum has erected a 250 yard long 2' 3" gauge track to demonstrate cable haulage in mining. The line itself is in the open, the very ends terminating in representations of a drift mine entrance. It has one car, built to mining proportions. The winding engine hauls a continuous cable which is attached to the car. So the cable runs in the centre of the track and to one side. At the far end the cable goes around a return pulley. The car is hauled away from the winding house by pulling on the side of the cable outside the track, which goes around the far pulley and draws the car away from the winding engine. For the return journey the winding motor is reversed and pulls the car back to the start. About a hundred yards of the track is visible from the car park without needing to enter the museum. It is the only opportunity of riding on this type of passenger transport in the country. Operation of the Paddy Train is restricted and may cease through inclement weather or staff shortages. Check before travelling.

Nearby
Sheffield Supertram is about 20 miles down the M1, while Manchester Metrolink is about 30 miles.

NATIONAL TRANSPORT MUSEUM, HOWTH CASTLE, DUBLIN

Address

National Transport Museum
Howth Castle
Dublin Road
Howth
Co Dublin
Ireland

Tel: 01 8475623 / 8480831
Gauges: 5' 3"; 4' 8½"; and 3' 0"

Open

Saturdays, Sundays and Bank Holiday afternoons September to May; daily June to end August.

How to get there

Public transport: Travel by rail to Howth Station using the DART. Outside the station turn right, walk a few hundred yards and past the church. On the left is the track leading to the Museum.

By car: Take the R105 out of Dublin towards Howth. The entrance road to the museum is on the right just before St Mary's Church. A sign is placed at the entrance road when the museum is open.

Photographed in very restricted space, Dublin United 253 has been restored at the National Transport Museum, Howth.

There is free parking provided at the museum.

Description

The Transport Museum Society of Ireland runs the museum, with no help from any state aid. The public are allowed in one of the two museum buildings (the other is a store for vehicles waiting for restoration). The museum has no tramway line, so the tram exhibits are all static. The bodies of two of the tramcars have been magnificently restored. In addition there are unrestored tramcar bodies, some on display and others not available to the public, being in store. The museum also houses a number of other road vehicles.

Trams on display or in collection

System	No.	Built	Description
Dublin United	–	1901	Director's car, 4 wheel, Open Top (in store).
Dublin United	224	1915	LCC T24 restored as Dublin 224.
Dublin United	253	1928	Bogie, double deck, totally enclosed
Dublin United	284	1928	Bogie, double deck, totally enclosed (in store)
Giant's Causeway	9	1889	4 wheel, single deck, unvestibuled
Hill of Howth	9	1902	Bogie, open top, unvestibuled

Nearby

Dublin and the new LUAS rapid transit system is about 5 miles west while Malahide Castle with the Fry model railway and tramway is about 5 miles north.

NORTH OF ENGLAND OPEN AIR MUSEUM, BEAMISH

Address

North of England Open Air Museum
Beamish
County Durham
DH9 0RG

Tel: 0191 370 4000
GR: NZ218548

Another tramcar that has recently been restored is Sunderland 16 at the North of England Open Air Museum, Beamish. Photograph David Cole.

Open

Daily Easter to end of October; closed Monday and Fridays from beginning November to Easter (check with museum for opening dates around Christmas).

How to get there

By public transport: travel by rail to Chester-le-Street. There is a bus service to Beamish Village.

By car: From Junction 63 of the A1(M) take the A693 towards Stanley via Pelton for 5 miles. Turn right after Beamish village to the museum.

Description

Covering 300 acres of ground this is a truly massive museum. The main feature is the reconstructed town, with period shops, houses and railway station. There are also separate areas with a colliery and pit cottages and farmyard exhibitions. To take visitors around the museum site there is an operating tramway with restored trams, and one replica tram (Newcastle 114 built in 1994 by W.G.H. Ltd), most from systems in northern England. The depot area not only maintains the running trams but also undertakes a programme of restoration, rebuilding preserved tramcars.

In order to do the museum justice it is best to allow a full day for your visit. There are a Victorian tea room and a souvenir shop.

Trams on display or in collection

System	No.	Built	Description
Beamish (Ex-Oporto)	196	1935	Bogie, crossbench, vestibuled.
Blackpool	31	1901	Bogie, open top, unvestibuled.
Blackpool	749	1907	4 wheel tower wagon trailer.
Gateshead	10	1925	Bogie, single deck, totally enclosed.
Newcastle	114	1994	Replica of 1901, 4 wheel, open top, unvestibuled.
Newcastle & Gosforth	49	1873	Horse car.
Sheffield	264	1907	4 wheel, balcony top, vestibuled.
Sheffield	513	1920	4 wheel, double deck totally enclosed.
Sunderland	16	1900	4 wheel, totally enclosed (awaiting restoration)

Nearby

The Tyne and Wear Metro is around 5 miles away north.

OXFORD BUS MUSEUM

Address

Oxford Bus Museum
Long Hanborough
Nr Woodstock
Oxfordshire
Tel: 01993 883617 (weekends), 01865 400002 (weekdays)
GR: SP440145
Gauge: 4' 0"

Open

Sundays and Bank Holiday Mondays throughout the year and Saturdays from Easter to end October.

How to get there

Public transport: Travel by rail to Hanborough Station. The museum is next door to the station.
By car: From junction 9 of the M40 take the A34 towards Oxford. After about six

miles take the slip road off to the roundabout marked to services. Take the right exit on to the A44 towards Woodstock. Three miles up the road is a roundabout with the A4095; take the left exit to Hanborough. A mile and a half up the road and you will come to Hanborough railway station. The museum is next to the station car park. There is ample parking at the museum entrance.

Description

This is an extremely well provided bus museum. The displays are nicely put together and show all different aspects of road travel, not just buses. In the collection are two Oxford horse tram bodies. They are awaiting restoration

Trams on display

System	No.	Built	Description
Oxford and District Tramways Co.	6	1881	Remains of 4 wheel double deck horse tram.
Oxford and District Tramways Co.	20	1881	Remains of 4 wheel double deck horse tram.

Nearby

The Vale and Downland Museum, Wantage, is about 15 miles south.

SANDTOFT TRANSPORT MUSEUM

Address

Sandtoft Transport Centre Ltd
Belton Road
Sandtoft
North Lincolnshire
DN8 5SX

Tel: 01724 711391 (24 hour information line)
Web: www.sandtoft.org.uk
GR: SE750083
Gauge: 4' 8½"

Open

For details of opening dates contact Brigg Tourist Information Centre 01652 657053.

Among the trolleybuses at Sandtoft are the bodies of two tramcars. Here Sheffield 419 is used as a tourist information centre.

How to get there

By public transport: travel by rail to Crowle station, which is six miles from the museum. Either do a long walk, or take a local bus to Sandtoft.

By car: from junction 2 of the M180 take the A161 towards Epworth. Take the first right (a minor road) signposted to the museum. Travel for two miles, and you will find the museum on your right with plenty of on-site car parking.

Description

This is Britain's biggest trolleybus museum. As the trolleybus was a development of the tram, early trolleybuses being called "trackless trams", there is interest for us. But more directly the museum also has two Sheffield tram bodies awaiting restoration. Both are on display and one is used as a display case for smaller items in the museum collection while the other serves as a Tourist Information Office.

Trams on display

System	No.	Built	Description
Sheffield	419	1920	4-wheel, enclosed top, lower saloon only.
Sheffield	442	1920	4-wheel, enclosed top, lower saloon only.

Nearby
About 25 miles north east is the Streetlife Transport Museum in Hull.

SHEFFIELD BUS MUSEUM

Address
          Sheffield Bus Museum
          Tinsley Tram Sheds
          Sheffield Road
          Tinsley
          Sheffield S9 2FY
Tel: 0114 255 3010
GR: SK379907
Gauge: 4' 8½"

Open
Saturday and Sunday afternoons, all year.

How to get there
Public transport: Travel by Supertram to Carbrook on the Meadowhall line. The museum is approximately 200 yards away in the old Tinsley Tram/Bus Garage on

Sheffield Bus Museum has its own Sheffield tramcar, number 460, which is being restored under the eagle eye of the shop window dummy.

the A6178 by the junction with Weedon Street, opposite the Tinsley Wire factory. *By car:* Going north leave the M1 at junction 34. At the roundabout at the exit of the motorway take the A6178 (follow the signs to Meadowhall shopping centre). At the next lights do not go right for Meadowhall, but stay straight on still on the A6178. Just before the next crossroads (with Weedon Street) the museum is on the right. Limited parking outside the museum.

Description

As its title suggests the museum was set up to preserve and display buses related to the Sheffield area. It does have one tramcar on display that is under restoration. While it is open at weekends, this is usually when members are working on the exhibits, it is suggested that your visit should be on one of the Special Sunday Open Days, when there are additional attractions. Note the museum is unheated and warm clothing is advised on cold days.

Tram on display

System	No.	Built	Description
Sheffield	460	1926	4 wheel, totally enclosed (lower saloon only).

Nearby

The Sheffield Supertram system is close by.

SOUTHEND PIER MUSEUM

Address

Southend Pier Museum
Southend Pier
Southend on Sea
Essex
Tel: 01702 611214 or 614553
GR: TQ894846
Gauge: 3' 6"

Open

Saturdays, Sundays, Tuesdays, Wednesdays and Bank Holiday Mondays, May to October.

As well as the exhibits in the museum, Southend Pier Museum has a cross bench tramcar on display on the pier itself. It was last seen sheeted over to protect it from the weather and vandals, hopefully the sheets have now been removed.

How to get there

By public transport: travel by rail to Southend Central station. From here it is a short walk (less than half a mile) down the High Street to the Pier.

By car: From Junction 29 of the M25 take the A127 to Southend or the A13 from Junction 30 of the M25. Once in Southend follow the signs to the Pier. There is some metered parking along the promenade. At the pier head go down the steps to the Pier Train station. The museum entrance is on the right. Note: There is a disabled entrance at the side of the pier via the open air amusement park on the west side of the pier. It is recommended to ring the above telephone number for the disabled access.

Description

The museum celebrates the history of the pier and the pier tramway. On the tramway the 1949 stock is probably the most famous and of the 28 carriages that were built five still survive. Of these the museum has been able to acquire four, the fifth being close at hand in the Lynne Tait Gallery at Leigh-on-Sea. The museum has three of the 1949 cars on display, with two earlier toastrack cars. One of these, the returnee from the Volk's Railway, is on the pier itself, though when I saw it recently it was sheeted over awaiting repainting. There is also a large model of a toastrack car that was originally built for part of a floral display in Chalkwell Park for the "Year of the Pier" celebrations in 1996. When the display was over the model was donated to the Museum. It stands in front of the restored pier signal box. The signal box used to sit half way along the pier. Also on show are displays of the history of the pier and of shipping associated with the pier. The museum has special exhibitions depicting different aspects of the Pier's history. Note that photography is not allowed in the museum.

Trams on display

System	No.	Built	Description
Southend	–	1890	4 wheel, trailer single deck, cross-bench
Southend	2	1949	4 wheel, single deck, totally enclosed.
Southend	7	1949	In store, no public access.
Southend	8	1898	4 wheel, single deck, crossbench, unvestibuled.
Southend	11	1949	4 wheel, single deck, totally enclosed
Southend	22	1949	4 wheel, single deck, totally enclosed.

Nearby

Do not miss out on the Pier Railway itself. Also nearby is the Southend funicular and a little further along at Leigh is the Lynne Tait Gallery with a Southend Pier carriage.

STREETLIFE TRANSPORT MUSEUM, HULL

Address

Streetlife Transport Museum, Hull
26 High Street
Hull
Humberside
HU1 3DX

Tel: 01482 613902
Web: www.hullcc.gov.uk/museums
GR: TA106290
Gauge: 4' 8½"

The Streetlife Transport Museum in Hull is a particular favourite of mine. Well laid out it has a replica street where the trams from Hull, Ryde Pier and Portstewart are displayed. Visitors are encouraged to enter the Hull car and examine the interior and try the controls.

Open
Every day all year.

How to get there
Public transport: Travel by rail to Hull Paragon Station. The museum is about three quarters of a mile from the station. Leave the station, cross Ferensway and enter James Road. This leads to the Queen Victoria statue. At the statue bear right into the pedestrianised King Edward Street and at the end continue slightly left into Alfred Gelder Street. Continue across to Lowgate, past the Crown Court and take the first left. You will find the museum facing you at the end of the road.

By car: The museum is situated in the old centre of Hull overlooking the River Hull. From the end of the M62 (Junction 38) carry on along the A63 via Hessle to Hull. After going past the marina and docks take the next left at the traffic lights signposted "All other attractions". Just before the swing bridge take the slip road into Market Place. Take the second right (a narrow road) to the High Street, turn left to the end and the museum is on the right. Parking is not easy. Alternatively leave the end of the M180 (Junction 5) and drive on the A15 to Hull. This crosses the Humber Bridge (toll) with superb views over the River Humber. When on the north bank at the roundabout turn left to the A63. Join the A63 towards Hull. Then as above.

Description

The new museum opened in 1989 to house the collection of historic transport vehicles. It is excellent and justly popular with adults and children alike. The three tramcars are displayed in a replica street. Visitors are encouraged to enter the Hull and Ryde Pier tramcars while the Portstewart steam locomotive is placed to allow good views of the internal workings. A first floor gallery allows the scene to be viewed from above. While in the Hull and Ryde Pier trams taped commentaries and conversations give a period atmosphere. In addition to the tramway interest there are large scale model steam locomotives, an early railway brake van and a signal box. Of the tramcars the Ryde Pier tramcar is said to be the oldest tramcar in Britain, being built just eleven years after the very first tramway in this country.

Trams on display

System	No.	Built	Description
Hull	132	1909	4 wheel, double deck, totally enclosed.
Hull	101	1924	Large model of 4 wheel, D/D, totally enclosed.
Portstewart	1	1882	Steam tram locomotive
Ryde Pier	4	1871	4 wheel, trailer, single deck, unvestibuled.

Nearby

About 25 miles south west is Sandtoft Transport Museum, while the cliff lifts at Scarborough are about 35 miles to the north.

SUMMERLEE HERITAGE PARK

Address

Summerlee Heritage Park
Heritage Way
Coatbridge
North Lanarkshire ML5 1QD

Tel: 01236 431261
Fax: 01236 440429
Web: www.northlan.gov.uk
GR: NS726655
Gauge: 4' 8½"

Summerlee Heritage Park has Scotland's only operating tramway. The restored Lanarkshire open top tram represents the local tramways, along with others from further afield.

Open
All year except Christmas and Boxing Days and 1st and 2nd January.

How to get there
By public transport: travel by rail to Coatbridge Central station. The Heritage Park is a short walk from the station.
By car: From Junction 5 of the M74 take the A725 to Coatbridge. After nearly three miles cross the A8 staying on the A725 to Coatbridge. After just over a mile, in Coatbridge, turn left at the junction with the A89 and follow the signs to the Summerlee Heritage Park. Turn right immediately after going under the railway bridge. The entrance is a short distance up this road. Free parking and free entrance.

Description
This is a modern open air museum (opened in 1988). It won Scotland's museum of the year in 1990. The 20-acre site shows Scottish life over the last 200 years, including a drift mine. There is also a $\frac{1}{3}$rd of a mile working tramway (the only working tramway in Scotland) connecting the entrance to other parts of the museum site. There is a small charge for the tram ride. There are also a number of Glasgow tram bodies awaiting restoration stored in and around the tram depot. When I last visited the Graz car looked rather strange in a purple livery, which had

been applied for the Queen's Jubilee. I was assured that there were plans to repaint it back into the green of Graz. A new acquisition had been the Glasgow Coronation car 1245, which is in need of restoration. The Dusseldorf car was being converted for disabled passengers and should be ready soon.

Trams on display or in collection

System	No.	Built	Description
Brussels	9062	1960	4 wheel, Single Deck, Totally Enclosed.
Dusseldorf	392	1950	4 wheel Single Deck, converted for disabled passengers.
Glasgow	1017	1904	4 wheel, Single Deck, Enclosed, under restoration.
Glasgow	1245	1939	8 wheel Coronation car.
Graz	225	1950	4 wheel, Single Deck, Totally Enclosed.
Lanarkshire	53	1908	4 wheel, Open Top, unvestibuled.

Nearby

A visit to Summerlee followed by a trip into Glasgow, a ride on the Underground and a visit to the Glasgow Transport Museum makes an excellent day out.

SWANSEA MARITIME AND INDUSTRIAL MUSEUM

Address

Tramway Annexe
Dylan Thomas Square
(Behind the main museum building)
Swansea Maritime and Industrial Museum
Museum Square
Maritime Quarter
Swansea
SA1 1SN

Tel: 01792 650351
GR: SS661922
Gauge: 4' 8½"

Swansea Maritime and Industrial Museum has a special tramway annex. Although not always open the annex has large glass windows and the trams are all easily seen.

Open
Easter to October Tuesdays to Sunday and Bank Holiday Mondays.

How to get there
By public transport: travel by rail to Swansea station. From there walk down the approach road to the Strand, and continue south for half a mile. At the end of the Strand turn right along Harbour Road into Victoria Road. Just past Swansea Museum you will see signs to the Maritime museum, which is set back behind the leisure centre. Total distance from the station is about one mile.
By car: From Junction 42 of the M4 take the A483 to Swansea via Port Tennant. After crossing the River Tawe follow the signs to the Maritime Museum.

Description
The tramway exhibits are held in the Tramway Annexe, which is behind the main museum building and near to the Dylan Thomas Theatre. The opening days for the Tramway Annexe are more restricted than the main museum. However, the building has a large glass front and all the exhibits can be seen from the outside of the building even if it is closed. The exhibits are all static, though there were plans at one stage to build a short operating line but nothing has come of this.

Trams on display

System	No.	Built	Description
Swansea and Mumbles	–	1956	Full size replica of 1807 horse car.
Swansea and Mumbles	7	1928	One end only of Double Deck, Totally Enclosed car.
Swansea Improvements	14	1923	4 wheel, Double Deck, Totally Enclosed, low bridge.

Nearby

The Oystermouth Model Railway Club layout is a few miles along the coast, and the Neath Gas tram at Cefn Coed Colliery Museum is about 12 miles north west.

TELFORD STEAM RAILWAY, HORSEHAY, TELFORD

Address

Telford Horsehay Steam Trust
The Old Loco Shed
Bridge Road
Horsehay
Telford, Shropshire
Tel: 01952 503880
GR: SJ667072
Gauge: 2' 0"

Open

Sundays and Bank Holidays, Easter to the end of September.

How to get there

By public transport: the nearest station is Telford, but that is quite some distance from Horsehay and the train services on Sundays are very poor.
By car: From Junction 6 of the M54 take the A5223 south towards Ironbridge Gorge. From the first roundabout you will see signs for the Steam Railway. After about 2 miles from the motorway take the second left at the roundabout after the Horsehay Village signpost. Drive through past housing on main road. The main road turns sharp left where straight on is a cul de sac. Immediately after the turn you will see the Old Loco Shed.

Description

Strictly speaking this is a preserved standard gauge steam railway. However, the abortive two feet gauge Telford Town Tram was moved to the site as an added attraction. The line is in a 'U' shape about 100 yards long and rides are given to visitors. The end of the ride is not far from the start! The standard gauge steam line is operated on the last Sunday of the month and there is also an 'OO' gauge model railway display. There is a small souvenir shop.

Trams on display

System	No.	Built	Description
Telford Town	None	1979	0-4-0 Steam Tram Locomotive
Telford Town	None	1979	4 wheel Open sided trailer

Nearby

The Birmingham and Midland tram number 12, converted into a chapel, is at the Blists Hill Open Air Museum, just down the road from Horsehay, but I understand that the museum has placed the tram into store, with no access to the public, while it awaits restoration.

ULSTER FOLK AND TRANSPORT MUSEUM

Address

Ulster Folk and Transport Museum
Cultra
Holywood
Country Down
Northern Ireland BT18 0EU
Tel: 028 9042 8428
Gauges: 3' 0", 4' 9", 5' 3"

Open

Daily all year except three days at Christmas

How to get there

By public transport: travel by rail to Cultra Halt (from Central station Belfast). The museum is a short walk away. Buses from Belfast also stop outside the museum.

Belfast 357 on display in the road transport building at the Ulster Folk and Transport Museum. Make sure you allow yourself all day to visit this great museum.

By car: From Belfast take the Bangor Road (A2) to just beyond Holywood, about 7 miles. The museum is well signposted, the entrances being immediately off the A2.

Description

The museum combines a vast open air area of reconstructed buildings in both town and rural settings which are on one side of the A2. On the other side of the A2 are two large halls containing the Irish Railway Collection and a collection of road vehicles. The trams are in the latter, though most enthusiasts will also want to visit the Railway Hall which has the Portstewart steam tram locomotive and exhibits from the County Donegal Light Railway. Near the exhibition halls is a miniature passenger carrying railway, though there is no operating tramway. All the tram exhibits are static.

The whole museum is superbly presented and has justly won many awards. Any visitor should set aside a full day to do justice to the displays. Cafe and souvenir shops are on the site.

Trams on display

System	No.	Built	Description
Belfast	118	1885	Horse car.
Belfast	249	1905	4 wheel, open top, unvestibuled.
Belfast	357	1929	4 wheel, double deck, totally enclosed.
Bessbrook & Newry	2	1885	Bogie, single deck, totally enclosed.
Fintona	381	1883	Horse car
Fintona	–		4 wheel truck
Giant's Causeway	2	1883	4 wheel trailer, single deck, totally enclosed.
Giant's Causeway	5	1883	4 wheel trailer, toastrack.
Hill of Howth	4	1901	Bogie, open top, vestibuled.
Portstewart	2	1883	Steam tram locomotive.

Nearby

The nearest other tramway interest is at the Giant's Causeway, a considerable distance away. Anyway you need a full day at least at Cultra to see it all.

URBIS MUSEUM, MANCHESTER

Address

Urbis Museum
Cathedral Gardens
Manchester
M4 3BG

Tel: 0161 907 9099
Web: www.urbis.org.uk
GR: SD835985
Gauge: Currently not known

Open

Daily all year except 24, 25, 26 and 31 December and 1 January

How to get there

Public transport: Travel by rail or Metrolink to Manchester Victoria Station. The museum is a short walk from the station. Out of the station turn right and walk

Britain's newest funicular and the only one inside a building is in the Urbis Museum in Manchester. The modern design suits the artistic nature of the museum's content. Photograph Mark Hows.

down the road. The Urbis Museum is the glass building ahead of you.

By car: Parking in the centre of Manchester is expensive and not easy. It is recommended that you park on the outer sections of the Metrolink system and ride into the city centre by tram to Victoria Station, then as above.

Description

The museum opened on 3 September 2003 and has Britain's newest funicular. The funicular is also unique in being the only one to be wholly contained within a building. The funicular is an essential part of the museum experience. After entering the building visitors ride up the funicular. As both the building and the funicular are constructed of glass, it gives a fine view over Manchester city centre. Once at the top, visitors make their way through the exhibits walking down the museum. The museum examines the experience of city living by comparing several cities on different continents. Currently reports indicate that the ride on the funicular is by far the most interesting part of the museum. At the time of publishing the entrance to the funicular is free.

Nearby

Metrolink Victoria Station is next door to the museum (which you should have used to get to Urbis); the Manchester Museum of Transport and Heaton Park Vintage Tramway are all close.

WELSH SLATE MUSEUM, LLANBERIS

Address

Welsh Slate Museum
Llanberis
Gwynedd
LL55 4TY
Tel: 01286 870630
Web: www.nmgw.ac.uk/wsm/
GR: SH580610
Gauge: Currently not known

Open

Daily April to October. Closed Saturdays from November to March.

How to get there

Public transport: Using public transport in North Wales is not easy. Travel by rail to Bangor, and outside the station is the bus station. Take a number 85 or 86 to

Not for passenger use, the Welsh Slate Museum at Llanberis has restored a typical Welsh slate incline to demonstrate to visitors how the funicular worked, with a loaded wagon pulling up an empty one. Photograph Mark Hows.

Llanberis. I recommend checking with Bws Gwynedd beforehand to establish the current bus routes and frequencies: phone 01286 679535.

By car: The nearest motorway is in England. So make you way to Llanberis, which is on the A4086 around 8 miles south west of Caernarfon. Llanberis is a small town and the Welsh Slate Museum is well signposted. It is between the Padarn and Perris lakes, in the Dinorwig Quarry and is part of the Padarn Country Park.

Description

This is not a passenger-carrying funicular, but has a unique place in the history of funiculars. Set in the dramatic Dinorwig Slate Quarry, the Welsh Slate Museum is a demonstration of slate working set in an operating quarry. Of interest to us is the restored and operational incline. These are early examples of using the funicular principle in an industrial setting. The remains of inclines can be seen all over North Wales and other parts of the British Isles, but none are working. The Slate Museum has rebuilt an incline to show how the funicular principles were used to transport slate down the mountain to the workshops. Entrance to the museum is free.

Nearby

The Conwy Railway Museum at Betws-y-Coed is about 20 miles east and the Great Orme Tramway is around 25 miles north east.

WINDSOR, LEGOLAND HILL TRAIN

Address

Legoland Windsor
Windsor
Berkshire
SL4 4AY

Tel: 08705 04040
Web: www.legoland.co.uk
GR: SU940748
Gauge: 3' 6"

Open

Middle of March to first week in following January, closed 11th & 12th November and 25th December.

How to get there

By public transport: travel by rail to Windsor & Eton Riverside station or to Windsor Central station. There is a shuttle bus service to Legoland from both stations.

By car: Legoland is clearly signed from either Junction 3 of the M3 or junction 6 of the M4. It is on the B3022 Windsor to Ascot Road, two miles from Windsor Town Centre.

Description

The Hill Railway is actually a funicular railway. Originally opened in 1991 as the "Central Africa Train" in what was then the Windsor Safari Park, the funicular seemed to have little future when the Safari Park closed in 1992. However, Lego purchased the park and converted it into the first Legoland outside Denmark. The Hill Railway was kept and the park designed around it. The track is around 1000ft long on a gentle incline, climbing about 100ft in height. On each end of the cable is a three-car train that runs on the single line. There is a passing loop at the centre.

Nearby

The Milestones Museum at Basingstoke is about 25 miles south east.

CLOSED AND PRIVATE FUNICULARS IN THE BRITISH ISLES

In order to give the complete picture of funiculars I have included this new section giving details of those funiculars that are closed, but are still recognisable and the few funiculars that have been built and used for entirely private purposes. They are not open to the public, but can be viewed from publicly accessible areas.

CLOSED FUNICULARS

BROADSTAIRS CLIFF RAILWAY

Address
> Albion Street
> Broadstairs
> Kent

GR: TR395675
Gauge: 5' 3"

How to get there

Public transport: Travel to Broadstairs station. From the station walk down the High Street towards the sea. At the 'T' junction at the end turn left into Albion Street. The upper station is on the sea side of the street in the back garden of number 14. The lower station is on the beach.

By car: From junction 7, the end of the M2 continue on the A2 to Canterbury. Here take the A28 heading for Margate. At Margate follow the signs to Broadstairs. Drive down the High Street. At the 'T' junction at the end turn left into Albion Street. The upper station is on the sea side of the street in the back garden of number 14. The lower station is on the beach.

Description

The Viking Bay Cliff Railway was unusual as it was constructed in a tunnel, running under the promenade. It had a single car counterbalanced by a concrete weight in a vertical shaft. Opened in 1910 it ran until 1990. Though repaired in 1991 a leak in the roof of the winding room damaged electrical equipment and the funicular remained closed. The line still exists, though by its nature only the upper

and lower stations are visible from outside. The lower station is the easiest to identify as it is on the beach, against the cliff wall. There have been continuing attempts
to raise sufficient funds to restore the line, but the money has never been forth-
coming. It is likely to be scrapped at some time in the future.

Nearby
The closed Margate Cliff Lift is only three miles away while the Folkestone Cliff
Lift is around 25 miles to the south west.

CLIFTON ROCKS RAILWAY, BRISTOL

Address
> Hotwells Road
> Avon Gorge
> Bristol

GR: ST575725
Gauge: 3' 8"

How to get there
By public transport: Travel by rail to Clifton Down station. From the station walk
straight ahead to Alma Vale Road. Turn right and walk across St John's Road, still
in Alma Vale Road. At Pembroke turn right. Walk along and take the second right
into Worcester Road. At the end is College Road, turn left and walk to the junction. Continue as straight ahead as possible into Clifton Down Road, then right on
to the B3129, the road leading to the suspension bridge. Before the suspension
bridge bear left into Sion Hill. Walk down to where the road curves right. On the
outer curve is a hotel. The upper station of the cliff lift is the flat topped low building ahead of you.
By car: From junction 18A on the M5 follow the signs to the A4 towards Bristol.
This road goes down the spectacular Avon Gorge. The suspension bridge is unmistakable. Just past it on the left, against the cliff face, is the lower station to the cliff
lift. There is no parking here, but a short distance on there is limited parking on the
left. To get to the upper station turn left into Granby Hill, which leads to Royal
York Gardens, and turn left into Sion Hill. Continue until you see the suspension
bridge and the road bears right. On this corner is the upper station; it is the low flat
roofed building.

Description
Set close to the spectacular Clifton Suspension Bridge and in the Avon Gorge the
Clifton Rocks funicular was built in 1893 as a four track system. It was unusual in

The Clifton rocks Funicular bottom station is easiest to find – even the name is written on the outside of the building!

being entirely within a tunnel, including both stations. Although popular to begin with the funicular suffered from declining passenger numbers and finally closed in 1934. However, the lower station building is instantly recognisable in the shadow of the suspension bridge. The upper station in Zion Hill can be found with more difficulty. It is well worth taking a few extra minutes to walk over the suspension bridge and marvel at Brunel's skill in designing and building a masterpiece of engineering, as well as admiring the spectacular views.

Nearby

The Bristol Aero Collection is about 30 miles north east; Seaton Tramway is around 70 miles to the south west and the Collections Centre at Nantgarw is 45 miles west.

Now almost completely hidden by the vegetation, the Falcon Cliff funicular is still in situ, though I was told that the instability of the cliff made its future very uncertain.

FALCON CLIFF LIFT, DOUGLAS ISLE OF MAN

Address

Palace View Terrace, off Central Promenade
Douglas
Isle of Man
GR: SC390770
Gauge: 5' 0"

How to get there

Public transport: There are two ways to get to the Isle of Man – by air to Ronaldsway Airport or by ferry landing at Douglas. The cliff lift is along Central Promenade. Take a horse tram to the Hilton hotel. The cliff lift is at the end of Palace View Terrace, a short cul-de-sac immediately past the Hilton Hotel.
By car: The ferry takes road vehicles and will land you in Douglas. Drive along the Central promenade for about a mile to the Hilton Hotel. The cliff lift is at the end of Palace View Terrace, a short cul-de-sac immediately past the hotel.

Description

This is the second Falcon Cliff lift. It was built in 1927 to provide an easy access from the promenade to the Falcon Cliff Hotel at the top of the cliff. The hotel became a non-residential public house and the cliff lift was closed in 1990. Later the hotel building was converted into offices and the cliff lift was offered to the Manx Government. Its future remains uncertain. In the meantime it continues to remain in situ, though very overgrown, decaying and vandalised. If in the Isle of Man it is worth going to have a look at, while you still can.

Nearby

In Douglas there is the Douglas Horse Tramway, which connects with the Manx Electric Railway which meets the Snaefell Mountain Railway at Laxey, also in Douglas is the Manx Museum. Across the island at Peel is the Manx Transport Museum.

The Cliftonville Lido Cliff Railway in Margate has long been removed, but the site is still recognizable. This is it during its operational days.

MARGATE CLIFF RAILWAY

Address

> Cliff Top Promenade
> Margate
> Kent

GR: TR350710
Gauge: 5' 0"

How to get there

Public transport: Travel to Margate station. Walk out of the station towards the sea. When you get to Marine Terrace turn right and walk to the road junction ahead. Take the left turn on the B2051, at the next fork bear right, still on the B2051 (Ethelbert Terrace). The fourth turning right is Athelstan Road. Opposite this road is the upper station.

By car: From junction 7, the end of the M2, continue on the A2 to Canterbury.

Here take the A28 heading for Margate. At the end of the A28, where the A254 heads right, turn left on to the B2051. Stay on the B2051 (Ethelbert Terrace) until the B2055 joins it. Staying on the B2051 look for the second right, Athelstan Road. Opposite this road is the upper station.

Description
The Cliftonville Lido Cliff Railway was another unusual funicular. It was built parallel to the coast line and not at right angles, which is the more usual way. At 65 feet long it was the shortest funicular in the British Isles and was used to encourage customers from the upper road to visit the Lido. It had a single car counterbalanced by an iron weight in a vertical shaft. Opened in 1913 it ran until 1972 and much of it has since been demolished. However, the site is still recognisable, with the vertical shaft for the counterbalance.

Nearby
The closed Broadstairs Cliff Lift is only three miles away while the Folkestone Cliff Lift is around 28 miles to the south west.

PRIVATE FUNICULARS
LIZARD RNLI CLIFF RAILWAY

Address
Lizard Lifeboat Station
Kilcobben Cove
The Lizard
Near Helston
Cornwall
TR12 7NQ
GR: SW715130
Gauge: 8' 0"

Open
The Lifeboat Station is open most days, but check beforehand if you want to see inside the station. The funicular is operated as and when required and is not open to the public.

How to get there
Public transport: The nearest railway stations are at Redruth, Camborne or

The first of the Royal National Lifeboat Institution funiculars is at The Lizard and takes crew down to the lifeboat and returns crew and rescued sailors back to the top of the steep cliff. It is unusual in having the motor fitted under the carriage. Photograph Mark Hows.

Falmouth, all some 20 miles from The Lizard. Travel from your chosen station by bus to the centre of The Lizard. The lifeboat station is at Church Cove. In The Lizard turn left into Beacon Terrace, then Green Lane, then second left into Church Cove Road. At the end of the road turn right to walk to the station at Kilcobben Cove.

By car: From junction 31, the end of the M5 continue on the A30 for 60 miles to Bodmin. Continue on the A30 for another 20 miles to Carland Cross. Here turn left on to the A39 through Truro to Helston. Then take the A3083 to The Lizard. The lifeboat station is at Church Cove. In The Lizard turn left into Beacon Terrace, then Green Lane, then second left into Church Cove Road. At the end of the road turn right to walk to the station at Kilcobben Cove.

Description
The lifeboat station at The Lizard is at the bottom of the very steep Kilcobben Cove. The stairway from the station to the top of the cliff made it very difficult to transport casualties up and supplies down to the station. A 45 metre funicular was installed into a new lifeboat station built in 1995. It has a single carriage which can carry casualties, the crew and supplies. The funicular is not open to the public, but the stairway alongside gives good views of it.

Nearby

Sennen Cove private funicular is around 35 miles west by road, while the Padstow RNLI funicular is about 45 miles north east and the Launceston Steam Railway is about 60 miles north east.

PADSTOW RNLI CLIFF RAILWAY

Address

Padstow Lifeboat Station
Little Gambia
Nr Padstow
Cornwall
PL28 8LB

Web: www.padstow-lifeboat.org.uk
GR: SW920760
Gauge: Currently not known

Open

The Lifeboat Station is open most days, but check beforehand if you want to see inside the station. The funicular is operated as and when required and is not open to the public.

How to get there

Public transport: The nearest railway station is at Newquay, some 12 miles from Padstow. Travel from Newquay to Padstow by bus. The lifeboat station is five miles away from Padstow, near to Trevose Head. It would probably be necessary to either walk or go by taxi.

By car: From junction 31, the end of the M5 continue on the A30 for 60 miles to Bodmin. Take the A389 through Bodmin to Wadebridge, another 9 miles. Here join the A39 towards Truro. About 3 miles from Wadebridge turn right on to the A389 to Padstow. From Padstow take the B3276 towards St Merryn, but before the town turn right to Trevose Farm (camping site). Continue on farm roads past the farm towards the lighthouse, turning right at the junction to the lifeboat station.

Description

The lifeboat station at Padstow is set against a steep cliff. This was a formidable obstacle for both the lifeboat crew and particularly casualties when returning from a rescue. Local people set up a fund to install a lift. This was opened in 1983. The lift was replaced over 1999-2001 with a single carriage funicular 35 metres long. The lifeboat station is open to the public most days, but this does not include travel

The second RNLI funicular is at Padstow and was built to make access to and from the lifeboat more straightforward. Photograph Mark Hows.

on the funicular. There is a stairway alongside (128 steps) that gives good views of the funicular.

Nearby

The Lizard RNLI funicular is about 45 miles south west and the Launceston Steam Railway is about 40 miles north east.

SENNEN COVE PRIVATE FUNICULAR

Address

Sennen Cove
Nr Lands End
Cornwall
GR: SW350260
Gauge: Currently not known

Open

This is a private funicular and is not open to the public, but is visible from the highway. Please respect the owner's privacy and property.

How to get there

Public transport: Travel by rail to Penzance. Then it is by bus to Lands End, or join a coach trip to Lands End and walk around the coastal path (northwards) the mile or so to Sennen Cove.

By car: From junction 31, the end of the M5, continue on the A30 for 120 miles to Sennen

This is the only example of a funicular serving a private house. It is to be found in Sennen Cove, Cornwall. Photograph Mark Hows.

Cove, a mile or so before Lands End. The hamlet is on the right as Lands End is approached. Go down the lane to the houses facing the sea.

Description

As far as I know this is the only funicular built for a householder. The funicular has a single flat car for carrying goods from the road to the house. It is not open to the public, but is visible from the road.

Nearby

The Lizard RNLI funicular is about 35 miles by road eastwards, the Padstow RNLI funicular is about 60 miles north east.

LISTING OF
HISTORIC TRAMCARS

I was very unsure what to call this section, or even how to select the tramcars for inclusion. It is aimed at being a handy guide to all the preserved tramcars. The difficulties of this are that there are many tramcars in routine operation that are far older than many preserved tramcars. For example in Blackpool the remaining examples of the 'Coronation' Class in Blackpool are generally recognised as special tramcars, yet they are far younger than most of the operational fleet. So I have borrowed the continental term of the historic tramcar to signify the tramcars in this section. The listing does not include normal service tramcars; for these look under Section 1, Operating Tramways, although some of the tramcars listed here may be used in public service, particularly at Blackpool.

Details of each tramcar are given under the current system livery of the vehicle. If the tramcar ran on other systems with their livery and possibly numbering this information is included, though you will be referred to the current system for full details.

Unless otherwise stated the tramcars are open to view during normal opening hours of the museum concerned.

Aberdeen District Tramways

1	Horse tram restored as a static exhibit in the Grampian Transport Museum, Alford.
54	In store, no public access.
70	Lower saloon used as summer house, no public access.
80	Lower saloon used a farm shed, no public access.
81	In store, no public access.

Aberdeen Suburban Tramways

11	In use as trailer, Alford Valley Railway, Aberdeen.

Amsterdam Tramways

474	Restored in operational condition East Anglia Transport Museum, Carlton Colville, Lowestoft.

Barrow-in-Furness Corporation Tramways

?	Body in store, no public access, Widnes.
?	Body in store, no public access, Widnes.

Beamish Tramway

196   Restored in operational condition, North of England Open Air Museum, Beamish.

Belfast Corporation Tramways

249   Restored as a static exhibit, Ulster Folk and Transport Museum, Cultra, Belfast.

357   Restored as a static exhibit, Ulster Folk and Transport Museum, Cultra, Belfast.

Belfast Street Tramways Co.

118   Restored as a static exhibit, Ulster Folk and Transport Museum, Cultra, Belfast.

Berlin Tramways

721039-4 In store, no public access, Crich Tramway Village.

3006   Restored in operational condition Crich Tramway Village.

The Berlin tramcar that was purchased by West Yorkshire Supertram (now Stagecoach Supertram) which was then passed to Crich Tramway Village and it is now in store.

Bessbrook and Newry Tramways Co.

2　　　Restored as a static exhibit, Ulster Folk and Transport Museum, Cultra, Belfast.

Birkenhead Tramways Co.

7　　　Horse tram. Restored as a static exhibit Woodside Pier, Birkenhead.

Birkenhead Corporation Tramways

20　　Restored in operational condition Pacific Road Museum, Birkenhead.

Birmingham and Midland Tramways Ltd.

12　　In store, no public access, Blists Hill Open Air Museum, Ironbridge.

Birmingham Central Tramways

?　　　Cable car awaiting restoration, in store no public access, Black Country Museum, Dudley.

Birmingham Corporation Tramways

107　　Awaiting restoration (lower saloon) Aston Manor Road Transport Museum, Birmingham.

395　　Static exhibit Birmingham Thinktank.

Blackpool & Fleetwood Tramroad Company.

2　　　Restored in operational condition Crich Tramway Village.

40　　In service on Blackpool Tramways.

Blackpool Corporation Tramways.

1　　　See Blackpool Electric Tramways Number 4.

2　　　Railgrinder in store no public access.

4　　　See Blackpool Electric Tramways Number 4.

5　　　In store, Crich Tramway Village, no public access.

8　　　Lancastrian Transport Trust, in store, no public access.

10　　Wokefield Park Training & Conference Centre, Mortimer, Reading, no public access.

11　　Awaiting restoration East Anglia Transport Museum, Carlton Colville, Lowestoft.

31　　Restored in operational condition North of England Open Air Museum, Beamish.

40　　Restored in operational condition Crich Tramway Village.

48　　Restored in operational condition Oregon Electric Railway Historical Society, Brooks, USA.

49	Restored in operational condition Crich Tramway Village.
59	In store, Crich Tramway Village, no public access.
114	See Blackpool & Fleetwood Tramroad Company, Number 40.
127	See Blackpool & Fleetwood Tramroad Company, Number 2.
143	In Store, Lancastrian Transport Trust.
144	Restored in operational condition Seashore Trolley Museum, Maine, USA.
147	Returned to Blackpool Tramways from Gerald R. Brookins Museum, Ohio.
159	Restored in operational condition East Anglia Transport Museum, Carlton Colville, Lowestoft.
166	Static exhibit, Crich Tramway Village.
167	Restored in operational condition Crich Tramway Village.
228	See Blackpool Corporation Tramways, 603.
298	In store under restoration. No public access.
304	Restored, Lancastrian Transport Trust, on loan to Blackpool Tramways.
327	See Blackpool Corporation Tramways. Number 663.
601	Restored in operational condition Rio Vista, California, USA.
603	Restored in operational condition San Francisco, USA.
606	Gerald R. Brookins Museum, Ohio,USA.
641	See Blackpool Corporation Tramways, Number 304
663	In store, Lancastrian Transport Trust.
717	Electric Loco, restored in operational condition Crich Tramway Village.
731	Restored in operational condition Williamette Shore Trolley, Portland, USA.
753	See Blackpool Corporation Tramways, Number 143.

Blackpool Electric Tramways Company.
4   Restored as a static exhibit, Crich Tramway Village.

Bolton Corporation Tramways
66   In service on Blackpool Tramways.

Bournemouth Corporation Tramways
13	In store Bournemouth awaiting restoration, no public access.
21	Awaiting restoration Wales. No public access.
31	In store Bournemouth awaiting restoration, no public access.
42	In store Bournemouth awaiting restoration, no public access.
53	In store Bournemouth awaiting restoration, no public access.
60	See Poole and District Tramways number 6.
71	In store Bournemouth awaiting restoration, no public access.
85	On display Museum of Electricity, Christchurch, Bournemouth.
86	On display, unrestored lower saloon, Aston Manor Transport Museum, Birmingham.

101   In store Bournemouth awaiting restoration, no public access.
106   Rebuilt as Seaton Tramways number 16.
113   Awaiting restoration Park Farm Museum, Milton Abbas, near
          Blandford.
126   See Llandudno and Colwyn Bay Electric Railway Ltd. Number 7.

Bradford Corporation Tramways
54   In store. No public access.
104   Restored as a static exhibit Bradford Industrial Museum.
251   See Sheffield Corporation Tramways Number 330.

Bradford Tramways Co.
40   Horse Tram. Replica built in 1992 by W.G.H. Ltd for Bradford
          Industrial Museum.

Brighton Corporation Tramways
53   In store awaiting restoration. No public access.

Brill
--   Snow broom. Restored as a static exhibit National Tramway Museum,
          Crich.

Bristol Tramways.
?   98-115 series horse tram, under restoration, Bristol Aero Collection.

Brussels Tramways
96   See Brill snow broom.
9062   In operational condition, Summerlee Heritage Museum, Coatbridge.

Budapest Tramways
2576   Four wheel single deck tramcar, private ownership, no public access.
2577   Four wheel single deck tramcar, private ownership, no public access.

Burton and Ashby Light Railway
14   Detroit, USA, in store.

Cambridge Street Tramways Company
7   Horse tram, in store Ipswich Transport Museum.

Cardiff City Tramways
131   In store, Crich Tramway Village. No public access.

Cardiff Tramways Co.
21   Restored horse tram Collections Centre, Nantgarw.
?   Remains of another horse tram Collections Centre, Nantgarw.

Carlisle and District Transport Co. Ltd
?   Tram in store awaiting restoration. No public access.

Castleberg and Victoria Bridge
3   Awaiting restoration. No public access. Ulster Folk and Transport Museum.

Charleroi Tramways
38   Trailer restored in operational condition Fintown-Glenties Railway, Co Donegal, Ireland.
41   Trailer restored in operational condition Fintown-Glenties Railway, Co Donegal, Ireland.
42   Trailer restored in operational condition Fintown-Glenties Railway, Co Donegal, Ireland.

Cheltenham and District Light Railway
21   In store Cheltenham awaiting restoration. No public access.

Chesterfield Corporation Tramways
7   Restored Crich Tramway Village.
8   Restored Crich Tramway Village.

Colchester Corporation Tramways
10   In store awaiting restoration. No public access.

Conwy Valley
1   In operation Conwy Valley Railway Museum, Betwys-y-Coed.

Cork Electric Tramways & Lighting Co.
?   29-35 series, in private ownership, no public access.

Coventry Corporation Tramway
71   In store awaiting restoration. No public access.

Cruden Bay Hotel Tramway
1/2   Restored Grampian Transport Museum, Alford.

Dearne and District Tramways.

?   Used as garden hut, South Yorkshire. No public access.

Den Hague Tramways

1147   Restored as a static exhibit, Crich Tramway Village.

Derby Corporation Tramways

1   Restored as a static exhibit, Crich Tramway Village.

Dewsbury, Ossett and Soothill Nether Tramways

?   In store awaiting restoration, no public access.

Douglas Cable Tramway

72/73   Restored in operational condition Douglas Corporation Horse Tramway, Isle of Man.

Douglas Corporation Horse Tramway

11   On display, Douglas Corporation Horse Tramway, Isle of Man.

12   Restored in operational condition Douglas Corporation Horse Tramway, Isle of Man.

14   Restored as static exhibit Manx Museum, Douglas, Isle of Man.

18   Restored in operational condition Douglas Corporation Horse Tramway, Isle of Man.

22   Restored as mobile shop Douglas Corporation Horse Tramway, Isle of Man.

46   In store, no public access, Birkenhead HeritageTramway.

Douglas horse tram 46 was on public view, but is now in store with no public access.

Dudley and Stourbridge 75 and Wolverhampton 19 under tarpaulins and Lisbon 361 in the open at the Black Country Museum.

47   In store. No public access.

49   In store. No public access (property of I. O. M. Railway & Tramway Preservation Society).

Douglas Head Marine Drive Ltd

1   Restored as a static exhibit, Crich Tramway Village.

Douglas Southern Electric Tramway Limited

1   See Douglas Head Marine Drive Ltd.

Dublin United Tramways

–   Directors' Car, awaiting restoration National Museum of Transport, Howth Castle.

22   In private ownership, no public access.

253   Restored as a static exhibit National Museum of Transport, Howth Castle.

279   In private ownership, no public access.

284   Awaiting restoration National Museum of Transport, Howth Castle.

291   In private ownership, no public access.

300   In private ownership, no public access.

317   In private ownership, no public access.

Dudley, Stourbridge and District Electric Tramways

5   Requiring restoration Black Country Museum, Dudley.

36   See Wolverhampton & District Number 19.

75   Awaiting restoration, under tarpaulins, Black Country Museum, Dudley.

Dundee steam trailer number 2 in store in Birkenhead.

Dundee & District Tramway Company

2   In store awaiting restoration, Birkenhead, no public access.

21   Steam Trailer. Restored in operational condition Crich Tramway Village.

22   In store awaiting restoration, Birkenhead, no public access.

Dusseldorf

392   Summerlee Heritage Museum, Coatbridge.

Edinburgh Corporation Tramways

35   Restored Crich Tramway Village.

79   Cable Tram in store awaiting restoration. No public access.

226   Under restoration Edinburgh. Access by prior arrangement only.

?   Upper deck, used as photo display exhibit, Summerlee Heritage Park, Coatbridge.

?   Upper deck, Summerlee Heritage Park, Coatbridge.

Exeter Corporation Tramways

19   Rebuilt as Seaton Tramways number 19.

Falkirk and District Tramways Co.

14   Under restoration. No public access.

Fintona Horse Tramway

381   Restored as a static exhibit, Ulster Folk and Transport Museum, Cultra, Belfast.

Frankfurt Tramways

210   Unrestored Birmingham and Midland Museum of Transport, Wythall, Birmingham.

Gateshead & District Tramways

5   Restored in operational condition Crich Tramway Village.

10   Restored in operational condition North of England Open Air Museum, Beamish.

52   Fire damaged in store, no public access, Crich Tramway Village.

Giant's Causeway, Portrush and Bush Valley Railway & Tramway Co.

2   Restored as a static exhibit Ulster Folk and Transport Museum, Cultra, Belfast.

5   Restored as a static exhibit Ulster Folk and Transport Museum, Cultra, Belfast.

9   Awaiting restoration National Museum of Transport, Howth Castle.

Glasgow Corporation Tramways

22   Restored in operational condition, Crich Tramway Village.

488   Restored as a static exhibit Paris Transport Museum.

543   Horse Tram restored as a static exhibit Glasgow Museum of Transport.

585   Restored as a static exhibit Science Museum, London.

672   Restored as a static exhibit Glasgow Museum of Transport.

779   Restored as a static exhibit Glasgow Museum of Transport.

812   Restored in operational condition, Crich Tramway Village.

1016   Awaiting restoration Summerlee Heritage Park, Coatbridge.

1017   Under restoration, Summerlee Heritage Park, Coatbridge.

1055   See Liverpool Corporation Tramways Number 869.

1068   See Paisley District Tramways, Number 68.

1088   Restored as a static exhibit Glasgow Museum of Transport.

1089   Restored as a static exhibit Glasgow Museum of Transport.

1100   Restored as a static exhibit, Crich Tramway Village.

1115   Restored as a static exhibit, Crich Tramway Village.

1173   Restored as a static exhibit Glasgow Museum of Transport.

1245   In store no public access, Summerlee Heritage Park, Coatbridge.

1274   At Seashore Trolley Museum, Maine, USA.

In somewhat cramped accommodation this Gloucester horse tram can always be viewed from the street.

1282   Restored in operational condition, Crich Tramway Village.
1297   Restored in operational condition, Crich Tramway Village.
1392   Restored as a static exhibit Glasgow Museum of Transport.
1   Works Car, in store, no public access, Crich Tramway Village.
W21   Works Car, in store, no public access, Crich Tramway Village.

Gloucester Tramways Co., City of
?   Horse tram under restoration Gloucester Transport Museum, visible from road at all times.

Glyn Valley Tramway Co.
–   Coach preserved at Talyllyn Railway.

Graz Tramways
210   Private ownership. No public access.
225   In operational condition Summerlee Heritage Museum, Coatbridge.

Grimsby & Immingham Tramway
14   Restored as a static exhibit, Crich Tramway Village.
20   See Gateshead & District Number 5.
26   See Gateshead & District Number 10.

Getting a rare breath of fresh air from its usual place at the back of the depot, Grimsby and Immingham 14 enjoys the sun.

Guernsey Railway Company
3   In store. No public access.

Halifax Corporation Tramways
82   In store. No public access.
115   Used as a shed. No public access.

Hastings Tramway Company
45   Awaiting restoration, Hastings Trolleybus Preservation Society, no public access.
56   Awaiting restoration, Hastings Trolleybus Preservation Society, no public access.

Heath Park Tramway
1   Operating on the 18" gauge line of the Whitchurch (Cardiff) Model Engineering Society.
2   Operating on the 18" gauge line of the Whitchurch (Cardiff) Model Engineering Society.

Hill of Howth Tramways
2   Restored (regauged 4' 8½") Orange Empire Museum, California, USA.
4   Restored as a static exhibit Ulster Folk and Transport Museum, Cultra, Belfast.

9   Restored as a static exhibit National Museum of Transport, Howth
           Castle.
10   Restored in operational condition (regauged 4' 8½") Crich Tramway
           Village.

Huddersfield Corporation Tramways
2   In store. No public access.
31/39   Under restoration. No public access.

Hull Corporation Tramways
96   Restored as in operational condition Heaton Park Tramway,
           Manchester.
101   Large model made in 1924 Hull Transport Museum.
132   Restored as a static exhibit Hull Transport Museum.

Ipswich Corporation Tramways
33   Under restoration Ipswich Transport Museum.
35   In store. No public access.

Johannesburg Tramways
60   Restored in operational condition, National Tramway Museum, Crich.

Krefeld Tramways
41   In store. Great Central Railway, Quorn, Loughborough.
412   In store. Walthamstow.

Lanarkshire Tramways Co.
53   Restored in operational condition Summerlee Heritage Museum,
           Coatbridge.

Launceston Steam Railway, Newport, Cornwall
1   Copy of Manx Electric Railway crossbench car used as carriage.
2   Copy of Manx Electric Railway crossbench car used as carriage.

Leamington & Warwick Tramway Company
60   Restored in operational condition, National Tramway Museum, Crich.
8   Horse Car. Under restoration Birmingham Railway Museum, Tyseley,
           Birmingham.

Leeds Corporation Tramways
W2   Works Car. Restored in operational condition, Crich Tramway Village.

6   See Hull Corporation Tramways, Number 96.
180   Restored in operational condition, Crich Tramway Village.
301   See London Transport Tramways, Number 1.
324   Lower saloon, in store, no public access.
345   In store, awaiting restoration, Crich Tramway Village. No public access.
399   Restored as a static exhibit, Crich Tramway Village.
446   See Hull Corporation Tramways. Number 132.
501   See Metropolitan Electric Tramways. Number 355.
526   At Seashore Trolley Museum, Maine, USA.
600   Restored as a static exhibit, Crich Tramway Village.
602   Restored in operational condition, Crich National Village.

Leicester Corporation Tramways
59   In store awaiting restoration. No public access.
76   Restored in operational condition, Crich Tramway Village.

Lisbon Tramways
305   In store North Wales, waiting to be stripped for Llandudno 7.
327   In store. No public access.
360   Waiting room, Derby Castle, Manx Electric Railway.
361   Left out in open, as delivered, Black Country Museum.
614   In store. No public access.
705   In store. No public access.
711   In store. No public access.
715   In store Millbrook, Southampton. Viewing by appointment 023 8089 4729.
730   Birkenhead Heritage Tramway.

Liverpool Tramways Company
43   Horse car. Restored in operational condition, Birkenhead Tramways.

Liverpool Corporation Tramways
245   In store, Birkenhead Heritage Tramway.
293   At Seashore Trolley Museum, Maine, USA.
762   Operational, Birkenhead Heritage Tramway.
869   Restored in operational condition, Crich Tramway Village.

Llandudno and Colwyn Bay Electric Railway Ltd
6   See Bournemouth Corporation Tramways. Number 85.
7   Under restoration Wales. No public access.

Liverpool 43, the restored horse tram, is only seen on open days at the Birkenhead depot.

London County Council Tramways

1	See London Transport Tramways, Number 1.
106	Restored in operational condition, Crich Tramway Village.
1025	See London Transport Tramways Number 1025.
1622	See London Transport Tramways Number 1622.
1858	See London Transport Tramways Number 1858.
?	Trailer awaiting restoration East Anglia Transport Museum, Carlton Colville, Lowestoft.
T24	Trailer in store Irish National Transport Museum, no public access.
T86	In existence, no public access.
T97	In existence, no public access.
T131	In store in parts, no public access.

London Street Tramways Company

39	Horse tram, part only, restored as display case, Crich Tramway Village.

London Tramways Co.

284	Horse tram restored as a static exhibit London Transport Museum, Covent Garden, London.

London Transport Tramways

1	Restored as a static exhibit, Crich Tramway Village.
290	See West Ham Corporation Tramways Number 102.
1025	Restored as a static exhibit London Transport Museum, Covent Garden, London.
1622	Restored in operational condition, Crich Tramway Village.
1858	Restored in operational condition East Anglia Transport Museum, Carlton Colville, Lowestoft.
2085	At Seashore Trolley Museum, Maine, USA.
2099	See Metropolitan Electric Tramways Number 355.
2168	See Metropolitan Electric Tramways Number 331.
022	See London County Council, Number 106.

London United Tramways

?	Horse tram, Caister Castle Motor Museum, Norfolk.
159	Type 'W'. In store, Crich Tramway Village, no public access.

Lowestoft Corporation Tramways

14	Awaiting restoration East Anglia Transport Museum, Carlton Colville, Lowestoft.
?	Awaiting restoration East Anglia Transport Museum, Carlton Colville, Lowestoft.

Luton Corporation Tramways

6	Under restoration. Mossman Collection, Stockwood Park.

Lytham St Annes Corporation Tramways

43	Lower saloon adapted for use by West Lancashire Light Railway, near Preston.

Maidstone Corporation Tramways

18	Awaiting restoration Dover Transport Museum, no public access.

Manchester, Bury, Rochdale and Oldham Steam Tramways Co. Ltd

84	Steam Tram Locomotive, in store awaiting restoration, Crich Tramway Village. No public access.

Manchester Carriage and Tramways Co. Ltd

L53	Under restoration, Heaton Park Tramway, Manchester.
W24	Eades patent reversible truck (body destroyed). Crich Tramway Village.

Manchester Corporation Tramways
173   Restored static exhibit, Manchester Museum of Transport.
765   Restored in operational condition Heaton Park Tramway, Manchester.

Manchester Metrolink
1000   Pre-production mock up of Metrolink tram body, Manchester Museum of Transport.

Manx Electric Railway
3   In store. No public access.
14   In store. No public access.
15   In store. No public access.
17   In store. No public access.
23   In store. No public access.
26   In store. No public access.
28   In store. No public access.
29   In store. No public access.
36   In store. No public access.
50   In store. No public access.
53   In store. No public access.
54   In store. No public access.
360   In store. No public access.

Melbourne Tramways
520   In private ownership. No public access.

Metropolitan Electric Tramways
94   Rebuilt as Seaton Tramways Number 14.
331   Operational, Crich Tramway Village.
341   At Seashore Trolley Museum, Maine, USA.
355   Restored as a static exhibit London Transport Museum, Covent Garden, London.

Modern Electric Tramways
01   In store, no public access.
3   Mr D Sorenson, Wilton, Connecticut, USA.
23   In private ownership. No public access.
225   Mr D Sorenson, Wilton, Connecticut, USA.
226   Converted into number 01 in 1965.
238   Mr D Sorenson, Wilton, Connecticut, USA.

Neath Corporation Tramways
1   Gas tram restored as static exhibit. Cefn Coed Colliery Museum, Crynant, South Wales.

Newcastle & Gosforth Tramways & Carriage Co. Ltd
49   Awaiting restoration North of England Open Air Museum, Beamish.

Newcastle Corporation Tramways
102   Operational, Crich Tramway Village.
114   Replica tramcar, North of England Open Air Museum, Beamish.

New South Wales Government Tramways
47   Steam Tram static display, Crich Tramway Village.

New York Third Avenue Transit System
674   Static display, Crich Tramway Village.

Northampton Corporation Tramways
21   In store. No public access.

North Metropolitan Tramways Co.
707   See Oxford and District Tramways Co. Number 20.
?   In store, Crich Tramway Village.

Norwich Electric Tramways Co.
39   Awaiting restoration East Anglia Transport Museum, Carlton Colville, Lowestoft.

Nottingham Corporation Tramways
45   Great Central Railway Ruddington Heritage Centre.
92   In store awaiting restoration. No public access.
101   In store awaiting restoration. No public access.
121   In store awaiting restoration. No public access.

Oporto Tramways
9   Horse Car. Operational Crich Tramway Village.
196   See Beamish, Number 196, North of England Open Air Museum.
273   Operational, Crich Tramway Village.

Oxford and District Tramways Co., City of

6   Horse Tram remains in store at Oxford Bus Museum, Long
           Hanborough, Nr Woodstock.
20   Horse Tram remains in store at Oxford Bus Museum, Long
           Hanborough, Nr Woodstock.

Paisley District Tramways

16   See Glasgow 1016.
17   See Glasgow 1017.
68   Operational, Crich Tramway Village.

Poole & District Electric Traction Co.

6   In need of restoration, in store, no public access.

Portsdown and Horndean Light Railway

8   In store, awaiting restoration. No public access.
13   In store, under restoration. Public access second Sunday in the month, City
           of Portsmouth Preserved Transport Depot, Broad Street, Old Portsmouth.

Portsmouth Corporation Tramways

84   Static exhibit, Milestones Museum, Basingstoke.

Portstewart Tramway Co.

1   Steam tram locomotive, restored as a static exhibit Hull Museum of
           Transport.
2   Steam tram locomotive, restored as a static exhibit Ulster Folk and
           Transport Museum, Cultra, Belfast.

Prague City Tramways

180   Restored in operational condition, National Tramway Museum, Crich.

Pwllheli & Llanbedrog Tramways

1   Horse tram, restored in operational condition Pwllhelli. Possibly actu-
           ally number 4.

Ramsey Pier Tramway

–   Petrol Locomotive in store. No public access.
–   Passenger Trailer in store. No public access.
–   Luggage trailer, Manx Transport Museum.

Sheffield 442 can be seen at the Sandtoft Trolleybus Museum.

Ravenglass and Eskdale Railway
—   "Flower of the Forest" 0-2-2 vertical boiler steam tram locomotive.

Rawtenstall Corporation Tramways
23   In store awaiting restoration. No public access.

Rotterdam Tramways
408   In store awaiting restoration. No public access.

Ryde Pier Tramway
3   Horse tram restored as a static exhibit Hull Transport Museum.
—   1889 Electric tram, restored as a static exhibit, Cothry Bottom Heritage
          Centre, Westridge, Nr Ryde, Isle of Wight.

San Francisco Municipal Railways
1226   Boeing articulated tramcar, in store Derby, no public access.
1326   Boeing articulated tramcar, in store Manchester, no public access.

Shane's Castle Railway
14   See Charleroi Number 38.
15   See Charleroi Number 41.
16   See Charleroi Number 42.

Sheffield Corporation Tramways

15	Operational, Crich Tramway Village.
46	Operational, Crich Tramway Village.
74	Operational, Crich Tramway Village.
189	Static exhibit, Crich Tramway Village.
264	Static exhibit, Crich Tramway Village.
264	Restored in operational condition North of England Open Air Museum, Beamish.
330	Operational, Crich Tramway Village.
419	Awaiting restoration Sandtoft Trolleybus Museum, near Doncaster.
442	Awaiting restoration Sandtoft Trolleybus Museum, near Doncaster.
460	Awaiting restoration Sheffield Bus Museum, Tinsley Tram Sheds, Sheffield.
510	Operational, Crich Tramway Village.
513	In service on Blackpool Tramways.

Restoration on Southampton Domed car 11 is further advanced than this older photograph would suggest.

Southampton Corporation Tramways

11	Under restoration Millbrook, Southampton. Viewing by appointment 023 8089 4729.
38	Under restoration Millbrook, Southampton. Viewing by appointment 023 8089 4729.
45	Operational, Crich Tramway Village.
57	In store Millbrook, Southampton. Viewing by appointment 023 8089 4729.
78	Parts in store Millbrook, Southampton. Viewing by appointment 023 8089 4729.
87	In store Millbrook, Southampton. Viewing by appointment 023 8089 4729.

Southend Pier Tramway

–	At Volk's Electric Railway Brighton (No 9), not running and not accessible by the public.
–	1890 Toastrack restored as a static exhibit Southend Pier Museum.
–	Awaiting restoration, Southend Pier Museum, was number 8 at Volk's Electric Railway.
2	Restored as a static exhibit Southend Pier Museum.
7	In store awaiting restoration. No public access.
11	Restored as a static exhibit Southend Pier Museum.
21	In store awaiting restoration. No public access.
22	Restored as a static exhibit Southend Pier Museum.

South Lancashire Tramways Co.

65	Awaiting restoration Manchester Museum of Transport.

South Shields Tramways Co.

?	See Douglas Corporation number 14.
?	See Douglas Corporation number 18.

South Staffordshire Tramways Co

?	1892 4 wheel truck (no body), Science Museum London, in store, no public access.
12	Lower saloon only, in store as "Gospel Car" at Blists Hill Museum, Ironbridge.

Stockport Corporation Tramways

5	Restored in operational condition Blackpool Tramways.

Sunderland Corporation Tramways

16	Awaiting restoration North of England Open Air Museum, Beamish.
100	See Metropolitan Electric Tramways, Number 331.

Swansea Improvements and Tramways Co.

14	Swansea Maritime and Industrial Museum (Tramshed Annexe).

Swansea and Mumbles Railway

7	One end preserved Swansea Maritime and Industrial Museum (Tramshed Annexe).
–	Replica horse tram Swansea Maritime and Industrial Museum (Tramshed Annexe).

Restored Wallasey 78 carries passengers on busy days at the Birkenhead Heritage Tramway.

Swindon Corporation Tramways
13   Under restoration. No public access.

Telford Town Tramways
–   Steam Tram Locomotive in operation Telford Horshay Steam Trust.
–   Trailer in operation Telford Horshay Steam Trust.

Vienna Tramways
4225   See New York Third Avenue Transit System number 674.

Volk's Electric Railway, Brighton
8   See Southend Pier Tramway.
9   See Southend Pier Tramway.

Wallasey Corporation Tramways
78   Restored in running order. Birkenhead Heritage Tramway.

Wantage Tramway Co. Ltd
5   Steam Locomotive 'Jane' Great Western Society, Didcot.

Warrington Corporation Tramways
2   Awaiting restoration. No public access.

West Ham Corporation Tramways
102   Restored as a static exhibit London Transport Museum, Covent Garden, London.

Wisbech and Upwell Tramway
7   Coach Number 7 awaiting restoration Rutland Railway Museum, Cottesmore, Oakham.
D2203   Diesel locomotive Yorkshire Dales Railway.

Wirral Light Railways
69   Operating tramcar Pacific Road Museum, Birkenhead.
70   Operating tramcar Pacific Road Museum, Birkenhead.

Wolverhampton and District Electric Tramways Ltd.
19   Awaiting restoration, under tarpaulins, Black Country Museum, Dudley.
34   Restored in operational condition, Black Country Museum, Dudley.
102   Awaiting restoration, used as waiting room shelter, Black Country Museum, Dudley.

Wolverhampton Corporation Tramways
49   Operational, Black Country Museum, Dudley.

Wolverhampton Tramways Co.
23   Horse tram, restored to working order, Black Country Museum, Dudley.

Wolverton & Stony Stratford Steam Tramway
2   Trailer under restoration, Milton Keynes Museum.
4   Trailer as farm shed, no public access.
5   Trailer upper deck, unrestored, Milton Keynes Museum.

Wrexham & District Tramways
4   In store. No public access, Wrexham.
6   In store. No public access, Wrexham.
?   In store. No public access, Mold.

Yorkshire Woollen District
57   In store. No public access.

TRAMWAY MAGAZINES

THE BELVEDERE ECHO
This is the newsletter of the London County Council Tramways Trust. Published three times a year it is sent free to all members of the Trust to keep them informed of activities and developments of the Trust and the associated organisation LCCTT (Promotions) Ltd. The latter has the sole purpose of raising funds to finance the tramway restoration of the Trust. See London County Council Tramways Trust in the Societies section.

BLACKPOOL TRAM VIDEO MAGAZINE
Published four times a year the video magazine covers current events and changes to the Blackpool Tramway system.
S.T.V.S., PO Box 13, South Shore, Blackpool, FY4 1TA. 01253 346005.

ELECTRIC RAILWAY JOURNAL
The magazine of the Electric Railway Society, sent free to all members six times a year. See Electric Railway Society in the Societies section.

FYLDE TRAMWAY NEWS
The monthly magazine of the Fylde Tramway Society, sent free to all members. See Fylde Tramway Society in the Societies section.

THE JOURNAL
The magazine of the Tramway Museum Society, issued free to all members four times a year. See the Tramway Museum Society in the Societies section.

MANX TRANSPORT REVIEW
The magazine of the Manx Electric Railway Society, issued free to all members. See the Manx Electric Railway Society in the Societies section.

NEWSLETTER
The magazine of the Black Country Museum Transport Group, issued free to all members three times a year. See the Black Country Museum Transport Group in the Societies section.

SCOTTISH TRANSPORT
Originally issued as Scottish Tramlines, the magazine of the Scottish Tramway

Museum Society, the title was changed when the Society broadened its interests to become the Scottish Tramway and Transport Society. Printing is approximately one magazine each year. See Scottish Tramway and Transport Society in the Societies section.

TRAMFARE

The magazine of the Tramway and Light Railway Society, issued free to all members six times a year. See the Tramway and Light Railway Society in the Societies section.

TRAMS

Published four times a year the magazine covers the history and current events and changes to the Blackpool Tramway. The subscription is £5 a year.
S.T.V.S., PO Box 13, South Shore, Blackpool, FY4 1TA. 01253 346005.

TRAMWAY REVIEW

The historic magazine of the Light Rail Transit Association. It is printed four times a year and is only available by subscription, £8.50 per year (£6.00 for current LRTA members) . Applications should be made to the subscription secretary Mr M. J. Lea, 23, Shrublands Close, Chigwell, Essex, IG7 5EA.

TRAMWAYS AND URBAN TRANSIT

First published in 1938 this monthly magazine has had a series of titles over the years. For most if its life it was called "Modern Tramway", which many people still use, then it became "Light Rail and Modern Tramway", and since 1998 has had the title "Tramways and Urban Transit". It is the Society magazine of the Light Rail Transit Association and is sent free to all members. However, it can also be purchased in many booksellers or by direct subscription. For details of the Society see the next section. Direct subscription is through:
Ian Allan Subscriptions Dept, Riverdene Business Park, Molesey Road, Hersham Surrey KT12 4RG.

TROLLEY TALK AND SCALE MODEL TRACTION & TROLLEYS QUARTERLY

These two American magazines are available in Britain by subscription to:
John G Neilson, 62, Broom Grove, Knebworth, Herts, SG3 6BQ.

TRAMWAY AND MODEL TRAMWAY SOCIETIES

TRAMS ON THE INTERNET

There are several egroups interested in British tramways.

For all UK tramways, subscribe by sending an email to:
uktrams-subscribe@yahoogroups.com

For the new Nottingham tramway system, subscribe by sending an email to:
NETTrams-subscribe@yahoogroups.com or visit the unofficial web site
www.nettrams.net

The Tramway and Light Railway Society has a site covering trams and model
trams. www.tramways.freeserve.co.uk

The Light Rail Transit Association has a site covering trams worldwide.
www.lrta.org

For information on funiculars the best site is www.hows.org.uk/personal/rail
The latter three also have many links to other interesting sites.

ASSOCIATION OF TRAMCAR RESTORERS AND OPERATORS (ASTRO)

This association was formed in 1988 to help and to coordinate the activities of the
various groups and societies involved in tramcar restoration and operation, and
most of these bodies are members.In short, ASTRO aims to help individual societies to help one another.

Tom Packwood, 21 Heathfield Road, Prenton, CH43 5RT

BIRMINGHAM TRANSPORT HISTORICAL GROUP

The group was formed to bring together all those with a special interest in the development and history of passenger road transport in the West Midlands. Members of the group collect material from all known sources to build up the most comprehensive picture of the development of passenger road transport in Birmingham and the surrounding areas. The major project is a full history of Birmingham's passenger road transport. Volume one covering the early years up to 1887 has been published and the second volume is near to publication. Photographic books of public transport in Birmingham, Coventry and Wolverhampton have also been published by the group. Anyone interested should contact:

Chairman BTHG, 62 Woodfield Road, Solihull, West Midlands B91 2DN

BLACK COUNTRY MUSEUM TRANSPORT GROUP

(Registered Charity)

Originally created to save items of road transport in the Black Country area the Group became a volunteer part of the Black Country Museum and helped build the tramway and trolley routes on the museum site. Group volunteers provide the bulk of the drivers and conductors as well as actively restoring many vehicles (automobiles and buses as well as trams and trolleybuses) for use and display in the museum. The museum has the only 3ft 6in gauge operating tramway in mainland Britain. A regular newsletter is sent to all members.

Black Country Museum Transport Group

Membership Secretary, 158 Yardley Fields Road, Birmingham B33 8QX.

BOLTON 66 TRAMCAR TRUST *(Registered Charity)*

The membership of the Trust consists of volunteers who, between the years 1963 and 1981 were involved in some way in the restoration of tramcar Bolton 66, which is running in service in Blackpool.

BRITISH HORSE TRAM ENTHUSIASTS

The British Horse Tram Enthusiasts aims to bring together all those interested in the earliest days of tramway when horse power dominated our roads. The group exchange information and undertake research about horse trams and are eager to help anyone with similar interests. There is also a very active restoration group who have brought back to life many horse trams seen in our tramway museums. The contact point is:

Rob Jones, British Horse Tram Enthusiasts, 103 Grove Road, Wallasey L45 3HG

DOVER TRANSPORT MUSEUM SOCIETY *(Registered Charity)*

Formed in 1980 the Society aims to bring together people with a common interest in transport associated with Dover. The museum has been created entirely and is run by members working as unpaid volunteers. The Society has preserved and restored many full size road vehicles, though not a Dover tramcar. The trams are represented by large scale working models operating on a layout. For further information contact:

The Dover Transport Museum Society, 33 Alfred Road, Dover CT16 2AD

EAST ANGLIA TRANSPORT MUSEUM

The Museum has been financed and developed by members volunteering their time and expertise. The wide ranging variety of transport includes an operating tramway and five tramcars. These are restored, operated and maintained by the members of the Museum.

Phil Carver, 26 Geoffrey Road, Norwich, NR1 3BG

Peter Davis, 33 Mayplace Road East, Barneshurst, Bexleyheath, Kent, DA7 6EA

ELECTRIC RAILWAY SOCIETY

The Electric Railway Society is the only society devoted to the study of all types of electric railway ranging from main line, to suburban and the new light railways. Monthly meetings are held in London and Birmingham and occasionally in other centres across Britain. The bimonthly society magazine, The Electric Railway Society Journal sets out to record all significant developments on electric railways in Britain, together with major developments across the world. Particular attention is given to news about the larger urban networks in the PTA areas and in major cities world wide.

Membership Secretary, 65 Hansom Place, York YO3 7FQ

FYLDE TRAMWAY SOCIETY

Founded in 1971 the Society brings together everyone interested in Blackpool's Tramway and transport system. The Society magazine, "Fylde Tramway News" sends members accurate and timely news of all events happening associated with the Blackpool Tramway. Regular meetings are held with topics of general tramway interest as well as focusing on the Blackpool system. Research is encouraged into the history of the Blackpool and Fleetwood tramways as well as actively supporting the current tramway system.

Membership Secretary, 330 Broadway, Rossall, Fleetwood FY7 8BA

GREATER MANCHESTER TRANSPORT SOCIETY

The Society was formed to cater for all those interested in bus services and fleet operation in the County. Members are active in bus preservation and the Society has become the supporting body for the Museum of Transport, Greater Manchester. The museum is owned by the Greater Manchester Transport Executive, but is run by members on a voluntary basis. As part of the historical context there are tramway items and models on display and they also work closely with the Heaton Park Vintage Tramways. Three tramcars are currently displayed at the museum. A regular bulletin is sent free to all members.

Membership Secretary, Greater Manchester Transport Society, The Museum of Transport, Boyle Street, Cheetham, Manchester M8 8UW

Tel: 0161 205 2122

LEEDS TRANSPORT HISTORICAL SOCIETY *(Registered Charity)*

The Society was founded in 1959 principally to ensure the preservation of three Leeds tramcars numbers 345, 399 and Tower Car number 2. All three are now at the National Tramway Museum. Number 399 and the Tower Car have been restored into service, while number 345 is in store, awaiting restoration. Interests have since broadened to include all other forms of local public transport. Many members own preserved buses and they welcome help in the restoration and main-tenance of the vehicles. The Society is open to all those with an interest in Leeds Transport. It has a regular monthly meeting, except in July and August, and a quar-terly newsheet. Members are actively involved in research into the history of public transport in Leeds. They have already published the first two volumes of a detailed history and are working to complete the story.

Honorary Secretary, Mr B Donald, 4 Maplewood Paddock, York YO24 3LB

LIGHT RAIL TRANSIT ASSOCIATION

The Society was founded in 1937 for the retention and development of tramways and light railways. It is an international body well known for its support of modern light rail transit. New members are welcome whether they be technical officers in the transport industry or interested amateurs. Members receive "Tramways and Urban Transit" each month and can buy major new LRTA books at reduced prices. Regular meetings are held in many centres and the LRTA arranges study tours. Members can subscribe to the historical magazine "Tramway Review" at a reduced price.

Membership Secretary, 23 Shrublands Close, Chigwell, Essex IG7 5EA

Web: www.lrta.org

LLANDUDNO TRAMWAY SOCIETY

The Llandudno Tramway Society is dedicated to collecting and restoring items relating to the Llandudno and Colwyn Bay Electric Railway for eventual display in Llandudno. The major project is the restoration of an ex-Bournemouth tramcar to create Llandudno and Colwyn Bay number 7.

Membership Secretary, The Llandudno Tramway Society, 12 Y Felin, Conwy, North Wales LL32 8LW

LONDON COUNTY COUNCIL TRAMWAYS TRUST

(Registered Charity)

Formed in 1966 (and known then as the LCC 106 Project) its initial purpose was to restore to fully working order a former LCC B Class open top tramcar of 1903. The tram was fully restored by 1983 and taken to the National Tramway Museum where it carried passengers once again. The second project was to restore a London Transport E/1 Class tramcar, number 1622. This was achieved in 1997 when the tram entered service at the National Tramway Museum. The Trust is very actively raising funds to restore the next tramcar, a 1902 London United Tramways open top Type 'W'. After that the Trust has a London County Council open top trailer car waiting restoration. The newsletter "The Belvedere Echo" is sent to all those donating to the Trust.

Secretary, 16 Baltimore Place, Bellegrove Road, Welling, Kent DA16 3LW

LONDON TRANSPORT HISTORY GROUP

The Group was formed in 1983 for the purpose of producing a history of the LCC Tramways, which was published in two volumes in 1989 and 1991 respectively. The Group then added the history of London Transport Tramways publishing the book in 1999. The Group intends to wind up when all stocks of the three books have been sold. As the active work of the Group has been completed it is not open to taking new members.

MANCHESTER TRANSPORT MUSEUM SOCIETY

(Registered Charity)

The main aim of the Manchester Transport Museum Society is the restoration of Manchester trams and the operation of the heritage tramway in Heaton Park. The Heaton Park tramway was opened in 1980 using a stretch of track that was originally the tramway sidings laid in the park by Manchester Corporation Tramways in 1905. The large tramway shelter (built in 1906), has been converted into a tram depot housing three trams. The building also has a small shop selling books and souvenirs, a museum and model tramway. The tramway is operated and maintained by members of the Society, who also restore the trams that run and will in the future run on the tramway.

Membership Secretary, 7 Marley Road, Levenshulme, Manchester M19 2SZ
Tel: 0161 442 7682

MANX ELECTRIC RAILWAY SOCIETY *(Registered Charity)*

Formed in 1973 the Manx Electric Railway Society brings together those interested in one of the oldest operating tramways in the world. The Society's magazine "Manx Transport Review" is sent to all members. Membership enquiries should be sent to:

PO Box 117, Douglas, Isle of Man IM99 1JS

MERSEYSIDE TRAMWAY PRESERVATION SOCIETY
(Registered Charity)

Founded in 1960 to save one of Liverpool tramway's bogie streamliner tramcars, number 869. After restoration in the Green Lane Depot at Liverpool and further work at the National Tramway Museum, Crich the tram entered passenger service at the museum in 1993. During that time the Merseyside Society acquired Liverpool horse tram number 43, now fully restored, electric tram number 762, under restoration, Birkenhead 20, again fully restored and Wallasey number 78, awaiting restoration. With the opening of the Birkenhead heritage tramway the MTPS moved to Birkenhead. Here members continue restoring tramcars and help to run the heritage tramway with its two Hong Kong built tramcars and the restored and running open top tramcar Birkenhead 20.

Membership Secretary, 7 Scafell Close, Eastham, Wirral, Merseyside

SCOTTISH INTERNATIONAL TRAMWAY ASSOCIATION

Formed in 1983 the Association had the aim of preserving and restoring Glasgow tramcar number 1016 and operating it with other trams from abroad on a heritage line in Irvine. When this fell through the tram was moved to Summerlee and a truck and electrical equipment have been acquired. Restoration so far has been limited and is overshadowed somewhat by the operation of the tramway at the Summerlee site. However, the Association continues to raise funds for continued work on restoration of the tramcar.

Details from:

Secretary, Scottish International Tramway Association, 87 Holmfauldhead Drive Glasgow G51 4PZ

SCOTTISH TRAMWAY AND TRANSPORT SOCIETY
(Registered Charity)

PO Box 78, Glasgow G3 6ER

SHEFFIELD BUS MUSEUM TRUST LTD

The Trust was formed to co-ordinate bus preservation in Sheffield and to establish a permanent museum in which to display them. The Museum houses the lower saloon of Sheffield tramcar number 460 which is waiting for restoration. It is believed that a suitable upper deck has been located.

Membership Secretary, 125 Guildford View, Sheffield S2 2NW

SOUTHEND PIER MUSEUM FOUNDATION

Formed in 1985 as the Friends of Southend Pier Museum, the society converted the old workshops on the pier into the current museum, which opened in 1989. The society helps with the restoration of the old pier trams and with other work in the museum. There is also research into the history of the pier.

Membership Secretary, 31 Castleton Road, Southend-on-Sea, Essex

STOCKPORT TRAM GROUP

The Group was formed to raise funding and to restore the preserved tramcar Stockport 5. Now that the tramcar has been returned to operational condition and is operating on the Blackpool system, the Group has focused its activities on the maintenance and upkeep of the tramcar.

Bob Hill, Secretary, Tel: 0161 928 8501

SUMMERLEE TRANSPORT GROUP *(Registered Charity)*

The Summerlee Transport Group is a voluntary organisation, set up to help Summerlee Museum run Scotland's only tramway. The group is involved in many different aspects of running a tramway, from the general maintenance of the fleet, to restoring preserved trams (currently Glasgow number 1017 is being rebuilt). Members can become as involved as much or as little as they wish. Many members are trained to become motormen/women and drive the trams for the benefit of museum visitors. There is also a very active tramway modelling group which meets on Wednesdays. There is a group 'OO' gauge model tramway layout which is taken out to exhibitions, while members also model in 'O' and 'G' gauges.

Membership Secretary, 104 Main Road, Condorrat, Cumbernauld G67 4AY

TELFORD HORSEHAY STEAM TRUST *(Registered Charity)*

This is primarily a steam railway preservation society. It has re-opened a short length of line from the old engine shed in the village of Horsehay. In addition members operate the two feet gauge steam tramway which runs in a horse-shoe around the picnic area behind the engine shed.

Telford Horsehay Steam Trust, The Old Loco Shed, Bridge Road, Horsehay, Telford, Shropshire

TRAMCAR SPONSORSHIP ORGANISATION *(Registered Charity)*

This organisation brings together those interested in raising funds to sponsor the cost of materials and contracts incurred in the restoration of specific tramcars at the National Tramway Museum. It is open to members of the Tramway Museum Society and members of the Organisation make modest monthly contributions to help build up the fund.

Treasurer Tramway Sponsorship Organisation, 3 Larkswood Close, Tilehurst, Reading RG31 6NP

TRAMWAY AND LIGHT RAILWAY SOCIETY *(Registered Charity)*

The Tramway and Light Railway Society was formed in 1938 at a time before many cities had abandoned their tramways. The purposes of the Society (a registered charity) include bringing together those interested in tramways, encouraging tramway modelling, collecting tramway and associated transport archives, photographs, drawings and other material. It is the only national society devoted to tramway modelling and members are active in making and exhibiting models in all scales from the very small ('N' gauge) to passenger carrying. There is an expanding number of area groups around the country with regular meetings and tram modelling activities. To promote modelling there is a models competition at the AGM each year. A society magazine is sent free of charge to all members every two months and includes items of modelling and prototype tramway interest.

Membership Secretary, 6 The Woodlands, Brightlingsea, Colchester, Essex CO7 0RY

Web: www.tramways.freeserve.co.uk

TRAMWAY MUSEUM SOCIETY *(Registered Charity)*

Originating from the Museum Committee of the Light Rail Transport League, the Tramway Museum Society founded and continues to operate the National Tramway Museum at Crich, Derbyshire. Trams from all over the country and abroad have been collected and restored to the highest standards for exhibiting and providing service at the museum. Society members provide volunteer assistance in all aspects of the museum, including tram maintenance and restoration, the public services on the site, all the necessary background infrastructure and the extensive and well respected archive and library services. The regular Society magazine "The Journal" is sent to all members.

Tramway Museum Society, National Tramway Museum, Crich, Matlock, Derbyshire DE4 5DP

Tel: 01773 852565

Web: www.tramway.co.uk

TRANSPORT MUSEUM SOCIETY OF IRELAND

The Transport Museum Society was set up in 1968 to develop and maintain a National Transport Museum in Ireland. The Museum at Howth runs entirely on the time and effort of volunteers. They run and maintain the museum as well as continue in the preservation and renovation of all kinds of Irish transport. Among the notable restoration projects have been Dublin United car number 253 and Hill of Howth number 9.

Transport Museum Society of Ireland, National Transport Museum, Howth Castle, Dublin Road, Howth, Dublin 13, Co Dublin, Ireland

Tel: 01 8475623 / 8480831 / 8392026

TRANSPORT TICKET SOCIETY

The Society was formed in 1946 to bring together into one association students of tickets and fare collection. The Society covers all aspects of tickets and ticketing systems, which of course includes tramway tickets. A monthly journal is sent free to all members.

Secretary, 81 Pilgrims Way, Kemsing, Sevenoaks, Kent TN15 6TD

Tel: 01732 761630

VOLK'S ELECTRIC RAILWAY ASSOCIATION

The aim of the Association is to bring together all those who have an interest in the railway. They are all actively assisting Brighton Council with the preservation, restoration and operation of the oldest electric railway in Britain. Volunteers perform a variety of jobs to give direct assistance to the operation and maintenance of the railway. It is believed that Volk's Electric Railway is the oldest operating electric railway in the world.

Membership Secretary, Fairfields, London Road, Hassocks, West Sussex BN6 9NE

Tel: 01444 235192.

MODEL TRAMWAYS

MODEL TRAMS ON THE INTERNET
The following Web Sites and egroups contain information about model tramways. They may also contain references to other web sites of interest:-
www.bec-kits.co.uk
www.blackpool-in-the-box.freeserve.co.uk
www.terryruselltrams.co.uk
www.tramalan.co.uk
www.tramways.freeserve.co.uk
www.tramalan.co.uk
For model tramways subscribe to the tramway modelling egroup by sending an email to:
Model-tram-subscribe@yahoogroups.com

MODEL TRAMS AND TRAMWAYS TO VISIT
Many toy and model museums contain models of trams. In my experience the vast majority of these have just a few poorly constructed OO gauge kits and one or two older tin toys on static display. They are not identified either by the system represented, the origins of the kit or the name of the modeller. I have not included these in this directory. The sites listed below have definite model tramway interest.

TRAMWAY AND LIGHT RAILWAY SOCIETY NATIONAL MODEL TRAM COLLECTION
The Tramway and Light Railway Society has a permanent collection of model trams in all scales to record the history and development of tramway modelling. Part of the collection is on permanent display at the Aston Manor Road Transport Museum, Birmingham. The aim of the collection is to show both commercial and amateur tram models to show the development of tramway modelling in both Britain and the rest of the world.

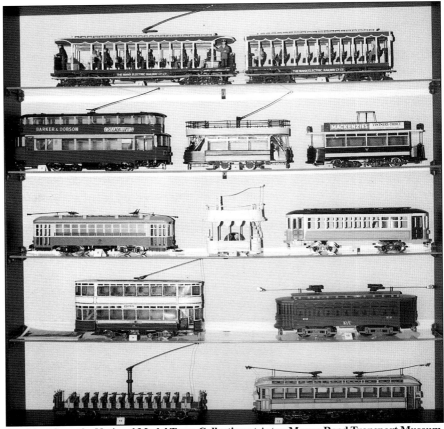

A cabinet from the National Model Tram Collection at Aston Manor Road Transport Museum.

ASTON MANOR ROAD TRANSPORT MUSEUM, BIRMINGHAM

Address

Aston Manor Road Transport Museum
The Old Tram Depot
208-216 Witton Lane
Witton
Birmingham
B6 6QE

Tel: 0121 322 2298 (24 hour information line)
GR: SP075904

Open

Saturdays, Sundays and Bank Holiday Mondays.

How to get there

By public transport: the nearest railway is Witton. Leave here and walk to roundabout on Witton Road (within sight of station), turn left, and you will find the museum on the left about 50 yards from the roundabout. Aston station on the cross-city line is ¾ mile from the museum – ask directions to Aston Villa Football ground. Walk past the ground keeping it on your left, and you will find the museum at the far end of the ground on the other side of the road.

By car: From junction 6 of the M6 (spaghetti junction) follow signs for A38(M) City centre. Leave at first slip road on left down to roundabout. Take right hand road (Victoria Road) to next roundabout. Take furthest right (B4140) to Witton. At next roundabout take right onto Witton Lane (alongside the Aston Villa football ground). Museum is immediately on left on entering Witton Lane. Free Car park alongside museum.

Description

The museum houses the TLRS National Model Tram Collection. Also the West Midlands Group of the Tramway and Light Railway Society have a small 'OO' gauge tramway layout on permanent display at the museum. It has a switch for operation by the public. There is also a large 1:16 scale model tram and trolleybus layout. The museum is a former tramway depot, originally for steam tram trailers and later for electric tramcars. The West Midlands Group of the Tramway and Light Railway Society meet at the museum on a regular basis. For more

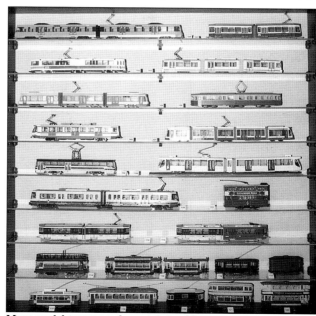

More model trams on show at Aston Manor.

information about the Group:
West Midlands Group, Tramway & Light Railway Society, 19 Park Lane, Sutton Coldfield, West Midlands B73 6DB
Tel: 0121 354 3201

For further information on the National Model Tram Collection contact:
TLRS, 9 Redwing Court, Kidderminster, Worcs DY10 4TR
Tel: 01562 68388

Nearby
The Midland Metro, Birmingham Museum and Art Gallery, Birmingham and Midland Museum Transport at Wythall, and the Black Country Museum with its operating tramway in Dudley are all worth a visit.

BIRMINGHAM MUSEUM AND ART GALLERY

Address
Birmingham Museum and Art Gallery
Chamberlain Square
Birmingham
B3 3DH
Tel: 0121 303 2834
Web: www.birmingham.gov.uk/bmag
GR: SP067869

Open
All year.

How to get there
Public transport: Travel by rail (or Midland Metro) to Snow Hill Station, turn right on leaving the station into Colmore Row, and walk to the end. This is Victoria Square and is recognised by the Council House and the statue of the large lady in the fountain pool (floozy in the jacuzzi). Walk past the Council House and turn right alongside it. The entrance to the Museum and Art Gallery is on the right.
By car: Parking in Birmingham is not recommended; not only is it hard to find car parking places, the municipal car parks are all pay and display, and if you overstay there is a very heavy penalty. So park on one of the Midland Metro Park and Ride stops and travel in by tram to Snow Hill and follow the directions above.

Description

The Museum and Art Gallery is widely known for its collection of pre-Raphaelite paintings. However, our interest lies in the Birmingham History galleries. In the galleries are two superb large scale (1:8) models of Birmingham tramcars. Number 1 is a bogie open top car and number 18 is a bogie balcony top car.

Nearby

The Midland Metro, Aston Manor Road Transport Museum, Birmingham and Midland Museum Transport at Wythall, and the Black Country Museum with its operating tramway in Dudley are all worth a visit.

BRADFORD INDUSTRIAL MUSEUM

Address

Bradford Industrial Museum
Moorside Mills
Moorside Road
Bradford, BD2 3HP

Tel: 01274 631756
GR: SE195379

Open

Tuesday – Sunday all year (closed Christmas Day, Boxing Day and Good Friday) open other Bank Holiday Mondays.

How to get there

By public transport: travel by rail to Bradford Interchange station. Take a bus number 896 from Interchange bus station which travels past Moorside Road. Alight at the Moorside Road stop and walk down Moorside Road to the museum. *By car:* From Bradford city centre take the Harrogate Road (A658) after 3 to 4 miles the Museum is signposted. Turn right off A658 into Moorside Road. Museum is 300 yards on left, free car park.

Description

In addition to the working horse tramway and the static electric tram and trolley-bus, the museum displays a collection of large scale models of Bradford horse and electric tramcars. These are in the same gallery as the tram, Bradford 104. Though the number of models is relatively small, the other tramway exhibits make a visit worth while and the whole museum is definitely worth a detour. It is possible to combine visits to this museum and the Shipley Glen cable tramway.

Nearby

The Shipley Glen Tramway at Saltaire is well worth a visit.

CRICH TRAMWAY VILLAGE

Address

> National Tramway Museum
> Crich
> Matlock
> Derbyshire
> DE4 5DP

Tel: 01773 852565
Web: www.tramway.co.uk
GR: SK345552

Open

Weekends throughout the year and daily from 1st April to 31st October. Disabled access and tram riding.

How to get there

Public transport: Travel by rail to either Matlock or Belper stations and catch local buses. Bus times on Busline 01332 292200.

By car: The museum is set in the beautiful Derbyshire Peak district. It is immediately below the tower Memorial to the Sherwood Foresters, which is a helpful landmark when visiting the museum for the first time. From Junction 28 of the M1 take A38 west towards Derby. After about 7 miles the Tramway Museum is signposted on right (A610). After another 2 miles take signposted right under railway bridge, climbing steep hill. 1½ miles to Crich village. Take right at crossroads, up hill to junction, follow signs to left, this road leads to the free car park of the museum. From Derby take the A38 east towards the M1. After about 10 miles follow signs left to Tramway Museum (A610). Then as above.

Description

The museum has a large exhibition hall set out to represent an early 1900's tramway exhibition. Amongst the full size trams are models showing other examples of tramcars. There are models by Bob Whetstone (1:8 scale), Felix Cunuder (1:12 scale), Frank Wilson (1:16 scale) and a 15" gauge steam tram locomotive and trailer by William Pritchard. There is added interest as some of the models are displayed in a cabinet constructed from the side of London Street Tramways horse car number 39.

Nearby

Nottingham NET is around 15 miles south east and Sheffield Supertram is about 25 miles north.

FESTIVAL OF MODEL TRAMWAYS

This exhibition is held in July of each year and consists of the finest model tramway layouts in the country, covering all scales and gauges from passenger carrying to 'N' gauge. Most tramway manufacturers are represented as are the major model tramway traders. The exhibition is held alternate years in London, at Kew Bridge Steam Museum and other parts of the country. The year 2005 exhibition will be at Kew Bridge Steam Museum. The nearest tube is Gunnersbury station. The museum is a ten-minute walk. Walk towards Kew Bridge and at the traffic lights, just before the bridge, bear right into Kew Bridge Road – the museum is on the right at the junction of Green Dragon Lane. Even closer is Kew Bridge Railway station – head for Kew Bridge and follow directions as before from traffic lights.

For further information contact:

Festival of Model Tramways, 216 Brentwood Road, Romford, Essex RM1 2RP

Web: www.tramways.freeserve.co.uk

FRY MODEL RAILWAY, IRELAND

Address

Fry Model Railway
Malahide Castle
Co Dublin, Ireland

Tel: 01 846 3779

Open

April-September daily.

How to get there

By public transport: travel by train to Malahide station. From the station the castle is well signposted and about a ten-minute walk.

By car: Malahide is about 7 miles north of the centre of Dublin. Take the R107 to Malahide. Once at Malahide the Castle is well signposted.

Description

Malahide Castle is a stately home open to the public. In a specially constructed building close to the main castle is the Cyril Fry collection and memorial layout. Cyril Fry spent his life building models of all types of Irish railed transport to the scale of 1:43 ('O' gauge). These include many examples of Irish tramways (from both the Republic of Ireland and Ulster). There is a static display of Cyril Fry models and a conducted display of the large model tramway and railway.

Set in its own grounds it is well worth spending time visiting the castle as well.

Nearby
The Dublin Luas and the National Transport Museum, Howth Castle are about 7 miles south.

GLASGOW MUSEUM OF TRANSPORT

Address
          Glasgow Museum of Transport
          Kelvin Hall
          1 Bunhouse Road
          Glasgow, G3 8DP
Tel: 0141 221 9600
GR: NS555667

Open
All year except Christmas Day, Boxing Day and 1st and 2nd January.

How to get there
By public transport: the easiest way is by underground. Leaving Kelvin Hall Station walk down Argyle Street towards the city centre. The Museum is in Bunhouse Road on the right.

By car: Park at one of the park and ride Underground stations, Shields Road, West Street and Bridge Street stations south of the Clyde and Kelvinbridge station north of the river. Then travel to Kelvin Hall Station and follow the above directions.

Description
As part of the magnificent transport collection the museum has a number of large scale model tramcars to illustrate trams that have not been preserved. So there is the double pleasure of seeing real trams alongside superb model trams. The only disappointing aspect is that none can be seen actually operating. While in the museum take time to visit the wonderful collection of ship models. If you are spending all day there, you can get refreshments and hot and cold meals in the cafeteria, which is worth a visit if only for the view over the tops of the tramcars.

Nearby
Glasgow Underground and Coatbridge Summerlee Heritage Park.

GRESLEY MODEL GROUP

Address
Gresley Model Group
Park Road
Church Gresley
Swadlincote
Derbyshire
GR: SK299190

Open
Public transport: It has not got any easier. Church Gresley is a small village in Derbyshire. The nearest railway station is five miles away in Burton-upon-Trent and there are no direct bus services to the village.

By car: The club house is open to the public on two occasions each year. Easter and early November, look in the Railway Modeller for more details. It is also possible for interested groups to visit by prior arrangement. Contact Keith Gulliver, 01283 223794.

Part of the 'O' gauge model tram layout built by the Gresley Model Group.

How to get there

It is not the easiest of places to find. From Junction 11 of the M42 take the A444 towards Burton Upon Trent (or from Burton take the A444 towards Nuneaton). Look for the "High Cross Roundabout". The roundabouts are all named at the top of the road sign. There are four roads into the roundabout, the A444 to Nuneaton, the A444 to Burton, a road to Castle Gresley and a road to Church Gresley. Take the Church Gresley exit (right when coming from the M42 or left from Burton). Follow this road (Castle Road) for some distance to a 'T' junction. Turn right to a roundabout you can see from the junction. At the roundabout take the left turning (Church Street, Church Gresley) and follow for some distance to the next roundabout (by this time the name of the road has changed to 'Commonside'). Take the left exit at the roundabout (Coppiceside). Park Road (an unsurfaced track) is the second on the left alongside the Barley Mow public house. The entrance to the club house is a short distance along Park Road from the pub, opposite the common. Access is through what appears to be a back yard.

Description

The extensive 'OO' gauge club layout, Worthington East, has a running 'OO' gauge tramway as a prominent feature, with a large looping circle around half the area and a spur going along the front of the layout. There is also an 'O' gauge tramway layout, Marston on Sea, laid along a shelf almost the full length of the club room. Most of the trackwork is dual gauge for standard and 3ft 6in gauge trams. The club room also has many photographs of the Burton and Ashby Light Railway. They were actively associated with the preservation and initial restoration of Burton and Ashby tramcar number 14, which spent some years in the yard outside the club house. The tramcar was taken to Detroit, USA for final restoration and is still operated at the trolley museum there.

Nearby

Crich Tramway Village is about 20 miles north east, while Birmingham is 25 miles south west.

MANCHESTER MUSEUM OF TRANSPORT

Address

Manchester Museum of Transport
Boyle Street
Cheetham Hill
Manchester M8 8UW

Tel: 0161 205 2122
Web: www.gmpte.gov.uk
GR: SD846007

Open

All year every Wednesday, Saturday, Sunday and all Bank Holidays except Christmas Day and Boxing day.

How to get there

By public transport: take the Metrolink to Woodlands Road stop. From there turn right and walk along Woodlands Road, and continue on Smedley Road. At the end of Smedley Road is Queens Road. Turn right and walk along until you reach Boyle Street on your right. Walk along Boyle Street alongside the bus garage until you reach the museum.

By car: The museum is 1¼ miles north from Manchester city centre. By car from the city centre follow the signs to Bury A665. The museum is signposted on the right when leaving the city. At the traffic lights turn right into Queens Road. Take the first left into Boyle Street. Drive past the bus depot and the entrance to the museum is at the far end. Limited free parking available. Contact the museum for a leaflet on visiting the museum by public transport.

Description

This is mainly a bus museum with other aspects of public transport including trams. Scattered around the museum are a large number of display cabinets with small scale (mainly 'OO') models of buses and trams. The display suffers from being too random to give any coherent story, but it is nice to see a selection of model tramcars. Again the lack of any informative notices means that visitors are left to their own devices to try and identify the origins of both the prototype modelled and the models themselves. An opportunity missed, but still worth a visit.

Nearby

The Manchester Metrolink is a short walk away. Ride it to Heaton Park Vintage Tramway.

MOSTYNS CAFE, LLANDUDNO

Address
66 Mostyn Street
Llandudno
Conwy
LL30 2SB

Open
All year.

How to get there
By public transport: travel by rail to Llandudno station. Follow the main shopping street (Mostyn Street) up to Lloyd Street on the left. The café is on the left just past the Westminster Bank.

By car: Llandudno is just off the A55 in North Wales. The most appropriate route is to turn off the A55 at Llandrillo yn Rhos onto the B5115 and then head for Rhos-on-Sea, and the approach to Llandudno follows the route of the former Llandudno and Colwyn Bay Electric Railway. Once on the main shopping street in Llandudno (Mostyn Street) proceed up to Lloyd Street on the left. The cafe is on the left just past the Westminster Bank.

Description
OK, what is a cafe doing in this book? Well you will be going to Llandudno anyway to see the Great Orme Tramway. While there go and have a meal or cup of tea in Mostyn's Cafe. You need to go upstairs to the first floor. Around the rooms, at picture rail height, is a 'G' gauge tramway on a narrow shelf with a backscene. Using proprietary LGB products there is a tram and trailer running around the rooms to entertain the customers.

Nearby
The Great Orme cable tramway is a little further up the hill.

OYSTERMOUTH MODEL RAILWAY CLUB

Address

Oystermouth Model Railway Club
Tabernacle United Reformed Church Arts Centre
Newton Road
Mumbles
South Wales
Tel: 01792 369885
GR: SS613820

Open

Saturday afternoons from the first Saturday in June to the last Saturday in
September. It is also possible for interested groups to visit by prior arrangement.
Contact John Peake 01792 369885.

How to get there

By public transport: travel by rail to Swansea station. In Swansea catch a bus to
Oystermouth (Mumbles). In the main shopping street of Oystermouth (Newton
Road) walk up past the police station (on the right) to the Tabernacle United
Reformed Church on the left at the corner of Chapel Street. Turn left into Chapel
Street and you will find the entrance to the Arts Centre on the left at the rear of the
church.
By car: From Junction 47 of the M4 take the A483 towards Swansea. After 2½
miles take a right turning onto the A4216 towards Mumbles. This road meets the
A4067 at a 'T' junction at the sea front. Turn right towards Mumbles. Continue on
the coast road to the first mini roundabout. Go straight across, still on the coast
road. At the second mini roundabout (where the shops are) take the right exit into
Newton Road. Just past the police station (on the right) the Tabernacle United
Reformed Church is on the left on the corner of Newton Road and Chapel Street.
The entrance to the Arts Centre is actually in Chapel Street.

Description

The Oystermouth Model Railway Club have built a large working 'OO' gauge
model of the Swansea and Mumbles Tramway in the balcony of the main church
building. The model represents the tramway running into Oystermouth and terminating at Mumbles Pier. In addition to the layout there is also a collection of colour
and black and white photographs of the tramway in its heyday.

Nearby

The Swansea Maritime and Industrial Museum is just a few miles away.

STOCKWOOD CRAFT MUSEUM AND GARDENS, LUTON

Address

Stockwood Craft Museum and Gardens and Mossman Collection
Stockwood Country Park
Farley Hill
Luton
LU1 4BH

Tel: 01582 738714
GR: TL087200

Open

Saturdays, Sundays and Bank Holidays all year (closed Christmas Day, Boxing Day and New Year's Day), also open Tuesday to Friday during April to October.

How to get there

By public transport: travel by rail to Luton station. From there walk to and through the Arndale Centre. At the other side walk to Park Square. Here there is a bus stop for route 1. Catch a route 1 bus heading for Farley Hill. Ask the driver to drop you outside the Stockwood Craft museum.

By car: From Junction 10 of the M1 take the short motorway spur towards Luton Airport. At the end of the spur, where it meets the A1081 there is a roundabout. Take the left exit (no road number) signposted to Stockwood Park. Take the second left then first left to Stockwood Craft Museum and Gardens and Mossman Collection.

Description

There are a number of collections and themes in this museum. The craft museum displays pre-industrial Bedfordshire and is supplemented with the Mossman collection of horse drawn vehicles. In the Transport Gallery (next to the Mossman Collection) is a superb model (1:16 scale) of the Luton tramway system. The layout is operated on special running days, contact the museum for details. Luton tramcar number 6 is also under restoration at the museum.

Nearby

The attractions in London are about 25 miles south.

VALE AND DOWNLAND MUSEUM, WANTAGE

Address

> The Vale and Downland Museum
> Church Street
> Wantage
> OX12 8BL

Tel: 01235 771447
GR: SU393880

Open

Tuesday to Saturday all day, Sunday afternoons. Monday opening during the season (check first for Mondays and for Bank Holiday openings).

How to get there

By public transport: travel by rail to Didcot station. A bus service from outside the station will take you to Wantage. From Wantage Market Place walk towards the church and turn left, and the museum faces you at the end of the road.

By car: From Junction 13 of the M4 take the A34 north towards Oxford. Turn off left onto the A4185 (signposted to Wantage). At the roundabout take the first left onto the A417. Stay on the A417 following the signs to Wantage. On entering Wantage follow the signs to the town centre. At the Market Place (you cannot miss it the road is one way around the market centre) take the first left (Newbury Street) once onto the one way system. Take the first right into Church Street and turn left into the pay and display car park. This car park has a strange 1,550kg weight limit, so check your car's handbook first! Walk back into Church Street, turning left. The museum is about 100 yards along the road.

Description

This is a very typical small town museum. But the town is Wantage and the Wantage tramway featured prominently in the development of the town and in tramway history. The museum celebrates this by an exhibit consisting of a replica of part of a tramway carriage which houses three large scale models and a video of a ride along the line (alas the video was out of action when I visited). The models are of the Grantham steam tramcar (the first self-contained steam tramcar in Britain), the Hughes steam tram locomotive (number 4) and a four-wheel passenger carriage. On the mezzanine floor is an interactive computer display. This was working and I found it slow and very simplified.

While in Wantage pop down to Mill Street to see the old Tramway Offices, now a shop but still with the Wantage Tramway Company name on the gable end. The steam locomotive number 5, officially known as "Shannon" but more popularly known as "Jane", is preserved at the Didcot Railway Centre, about 8 miles east of Wantage.

Nearby
The Oxford Bus Museum is about 20 miles north.

MODEL TRAMWAY SUPPLIERS

KIT MANUFACTURERS

ABS Kits

An expanding range of white metal British outline tramcars kits in 'OO' gauge, plus motorised 4 wheel chassis kits. Send £1 plus SAE for catalogue.
36 Field Barn Drive, Weymouth, Dorset DTI ED

ALPHAGRAPHIX

A wide and ever increasing range of 'HO', 'OO' and 'O' gauge full colour card kits of British and continental tramcars. Send 4 x 1st class stamps for illustrated catalogue.
23 Darris Road, Selly Park, Birmingham B29 7QY.

BEC KITS

A wide range of continental and American tramcar kits in 'HO' gauge, plus ready-to-run 4 wheel and bogie mechanisms and a range of British outline tram parts in 4mm scale. They have also taken over the "Tower Trams" range of plastic 'OO' kits. They also supply overhead parts in 'N', 'HO', 'O' and 'G' scales. Mail order only. Send SAE for price list.
47 Woodlands Road, Lancaster LA1 2EH
Web: www.bec-kits.co.uk

BLACKPOOL IN THE BOX

Various model tram items, particularly to assist motorising die cast tram models and 4mm scale transfers.
P O Box 147, Plymouth, Devon PL2 1YX
Web: www.blackpool-in-the-box.freeserve.co.uk

BLACKPOOL PLASTICS

Blackpool Plastics have recently sold their business and details of the new owner are not available. They were the manufacturers of the Blackpool plastic 'OO' gauge kits formerly manufactured by Hadfields. The range has only tramcars that run or ran in Blackpool, but are also very useful for conversion to other systems' tramcars. See suppliers.

CORGI MODELS

Die cast models of tramcars. The Blackpool and London ranges are made to 'OO' gauge. The older 4 wheel tramcars are made to a larger scale and are not suitable for mixing with 'OO' scale models. See suppliers.

EFE MODELS

Die cast model of the Leeds Horsfield tramcar in 'OO' gauge. A variety of liveries have been produced. No longer in production, they can be found second-hand. See suppliers.

KNIGHTWING PLASTIC KITS

The ex-Keil Kraft plastic kit of the Edinburgh 4 wheel standard tramcar. See suppliers.

MARK HUGHES

Two white metal 4mm scale tramcar kits of the Manx Electric 3' 0" gauge bogie saloon tramcar and the Manchester Metrolink articulated tramcar. There is also an etched brass kit of the Blackpool double deck tramcar number 761. Catalogue price £1 plus 9" by 4" SAE (overseas 5 International Reply Coupons).
Mark Hughes, 23 Orchard Rise, Tibberton, Gloucester GL19 3AT

MERSEYSIDE TRANSPORT PRESERVATION GROUP

Two white metal kits of Liverpool tramcars. A 4 wheel Priestly tramcar and a conversion kit for a Bellamy Roof tramcar. See suppliers.

P. D. MARSH

One white metal kit in 'OO' gauge of the Black Country 'Tividale' tramcar. See suppliers.

NU-CAST

One white metal kit in 'OO' gauge of the Wisbech and Upwell steam tram locomotive. The 4 wheel London MET class 'E' is also available only from Derek Lambelle. See suppliers.

ROXEY MOULDINGS

One white metal kit of the Hellingley Hospital tramway locomotive in 'OO' gauge. See suppliers.

TERRY RUSSELL TRAMS

Manufacturers of 'O' gauge tramcar parts, ready to run motorised chassis and bogies and working trolley poles and overhead. Terry Russell also supplies the biggest range of tramcar drawings in 1:32 scale, 7mm scale gauge and 4mm scale. He also sells card tramcar and building kits in OO and O gauge. Latest addition to the range, the 7mm scale etched brass kit for a London Transport E/1 tramcar. Mail order only. Send 4 x 1st class stamps (Overseas, 4 International Reply Coupons) for full catalogue.

Mr Terry Russell, 'Chaceside', St Leonards Park, Horsham, West Sussex RH13 6EG

Web: www.terryruselltrams.co.uk

TOWER TRAMS

Merged with Bec Kits they manufacture a number of 'OO' gauge plastic kits of British tramcars. Again the kits are not only good to make as intended but also provide all kinds of parts for conversion into other tramcars. Mail order only. Send SAE for price list.

47 Woodlands Road, Lancaster, LA1 2EH

Web: www.bec-kits.co.uk

TRAMALAN

Manufacturers of the largest range of white metal kits of British 'OO' gauge trams and trams from all over the world in 'HO' gauge. They also make an ever-increasing selection of conversion kits to easily change an existing plastic kit into a quite different tramcar. Mail order only. 6 x 1st class stamps for illustrated catalogue.

P O Box 2, Blackpool FY3 8DZ

Web: www.tramalan.co.uk

DAVID VOICE

Supplies the ex-PC range of overhead wire, etched brass overhead and tramcar parts in 'O' and 'OO' gauges and chassis kits in 'OO' gauge. Mail order only. Send SAE for price list.

9 Redwing Court, Kidderminster, Worcs DY10 4TR

e-mail: d.voice2@btinternet.com

SELECTED BOOKSELLERS OF TRAMWAY LITERATURE

CRICH TRAMWAY MUSEUM BOOKSHOP

The Bookshop at Crich has a wide range of new tramway books from Britain and abroad. Visitors to the Museum can see all the books on display.

The Bookshop, National Tramway Museum, Crich, Derbyshire DE4 5DP. Tel: 01773 852565. Fax: 01773 852326.

ROBERT HUMM & CO., TRANSPORT BOOKSELLERS

Usually 500+ old and out-of-print tramway books in stock. No lists, better quality items often included in our railway catalogues. Always ready to purchase antiquarian or scarce tramway literature, British and foreign.

Station House, Gresley Drive, Stamford, Lincolnshire, PE9 2JN.

Tel: 01780-766266; Fax: 01780-757929

Shop open 9.30 to 5.30 Mon-Sat. Customer parking.

ADAM GORDON

Postal business. Huge stocks of second-hand tramway and transport-related literature. Please send stamped addressed envelope for list (issued three or four times a year).

Kintradwell Farmhouse, Brora, Sutherland KW9 6LU

Tel 01408 622660

e-mail: adam@adamgordon.freewire.co.uk

INDEX

We have confined the index to the principal names of operators, museums and geographical locations; (some names may appear twice where the location is not always obvious). Only the first page of the subject is entered:

More Transport Titles in the Adam Gordon Collection

A History of the British Steam Tram

David Gladwin. Hardback, B4, 180pp inc. covers, £40. Print-run limited to 650.

Chapter titles are: Preamble [the social scene]; 1870 and All That [legislation, and early steam buses]; Trams and Traps ["workers versus wealth", The Birmingham & Aston Tramways and local opposition]; Pros and Cons – and Early Days [analysis of problems in the early days of steam, highlighting the Birmingham area]; Travails of a tram engine [study of the mechanics of tram engines, and also of the composition of rails and the effects of wheels thereon]; Manufacturers [the principal players: Wilkinson, Beyer Peacock, Black Hawthorn, Thomas Green, Hughes/Falcon/Brush, Kitson, Manning Wardle, and Merryweather]; Digressions [odd-bods (smaller manufacturers + non-steam engines): Mékarski, Brunner, Dick Kerr, Fireless, Fox Walker, Franco-Belge, Grantham, Hydroleum, Krauss, Matthews, Prima Donna, Serpollet, SNCF, Telford, Winterthur, and Woods]; People Carriers [principal trailer manufacturers, including walk-round tour of the Britannia Works of Brown Marshalls]; Lifeguards and Lights [mostly lifeguards and patents]; Permanent Way [fascinating step by step account of how the PW is laid, detailing the essential tools, as seen through the eyes of an apprentice].

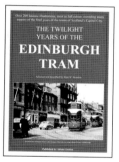

The Twilight Years of the Edinburgh Tram

Alan Brotchie. Softback, A4, 194 photographs, including 152 in colour, 112pp, £25.

"...the author has done well to assemble so many views in colour ... the book is a worthy reminder of a fine tramway system that should never have been destroyed." [Tramway Review]

"...the descriptive captions are highly appropriate, and provide a neat yet clear and comprehensive overview of the system's closing years ... the quality of both content and production are sufficient advertisement." [TMS Journal]

The Twilight Years of the Glasgow Tram

Softback, 144 pages, £25.

Contains over 250 coloured pictures taken by Douglas McMillan, selected, prefaced and captioned by Alasdair Turnbull, who has maintained a humorous and homely commentary on a clockwise tour of the Glasgow system as it was in the 1950's and early 1960's. Published to celebrate the centenary of the introduction of electric traction to the Glasgow tramways on 13th October 1898.

"Every so often one comes across a book which is almost beyond compare, and this is one such. More, it is sure to set a new standard for albums, and one to which every author and publisher might do well to aspire...a wonderful book..." [Tramway Museum Society Journal]

The Twilight Years of the Trams in Aberdeen and Dundee

Softback, 120pp, 231 illustrations, mostly coloured, with captions and Introduction by Alan Brotchie, £25

Includes photographs from 30 different sources.

"Congratulations on the high quality of printing and production. Very impressive." [AG, Bradford]

"This volume follows the style and the standard of earlier works on the Glasgow and Edinburgh trams and, hard though it may be to believe, surpasses those earlier works. The first impression is of fantastic quality in the reproduction of the photographs..." [TMS Journal]

Toy and Model Trams of the World, Volume 1

Gottfried Kuře and David Voice, 128pp, A4, all colour, £25.

[Back cover comment]: "Following a lifetime of modelling and collecting small trams (the authors) have teamed up to pool their knowledge in this definitive work describing toy and model trams, trolleybuses and underground trains from over the whole world. In volume I the authors look at toy trams, all die cast small trams and the vast souvenir market. The book gives invaluable tips about collecting and looking after toy trams, then covers historical tinplate, tinplate after 1950, wood, card, die cast, plastic, all other materials, souvenirs and children's toys. To help identify items there is a manufacturers' index and around 400 illustrations, mainly full colour photographs. Over 1,800 individual small trams, trolleybuses and underground trains are included and there are around 480 manufacturers' names, most entries having an historical summary. The book also guides the collector with market price estimates for toy trams no longer in production."

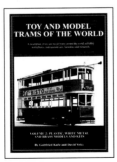

Toy and Model Trams of the World, Volume 2

Plastic, White Metal and Brass Models and Kits. Gottfied Kuře and David Voice, A4 softback, 188pp, £30.

[Back cover comment]: "Once again Gottfried Kuře and David Voice have teamed up to pool their knowledge in this definitive work describing models and kits of trams, trolleybuses, underground trains, funiculars and monorails from all over the world. Volume 2 takes the story from Volume 1 and looks at the vast range of models and kits that have been produced from countries all over the world. The introduction looks at the various scales and gauges in use, then the three main manufacturing materials: plastic, white metal and brass. The final chapter looks back to Volume 1 and adds new information that has come to light since its publication. To help identify models the book contains an index of manufacturers for both volumes and there are around 600 full colour photographs. Around 4,000 individual model trams and kits are identified, with the listing in each chapter being alphabetical by manufacturer. There are around 1,000 manufacturers named, most having a historical summary."

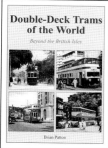

Double Deck Trams of the World, Beyond the British Isles

Brian Patton, A4 softback, 180pp, covers coloured both sides, £18.

"Patton has searched far and wide for his material, down to the photographic record of the only double-decker ever to run in Zurich. The date of operation was 1 April 1912 and even the reputedly dour Swiss have a sense of humour, I suspect." [Tramfare] "The illustrations are well reproduced and include some fascinating, animated views from the impressive but seldom-illustrated collection of Pam Eaton. This book endeavours to be a complete survey of overseas double-deck electric cars and necessarily only an overview of other means of propulsion, but it is unlikely ever to superseded except by an updated edition by the same author. It well merits a place on the bookshelf of any tramway student with a catholic interest in this form of design. [Tramways & Urban Transit]

Clippie

Z. Katin, a few months in the life of a tram and bus conductress in the war in Sheffield, 124pp, softback, reprint, £7

"When I was married, at the age of 22, I tried for a long time to obtain work. At the end of 18 years' interrupted effort I succeeded. The second world war had made its debut just as I had resigned myself to the knowledge that in Britain a married woman may not work outside her home except as a charlady.

Soon after my husband was called up and my son had turned 14 there came a request from the Minister of Labour and National Service that I call at the employment exchange and there be directed to work of national importance. I was not thrilled. My desire to help in the war effort was tinged with a resentment that society could only find work for me in a period of destruction and sudden death, and then only by resorting to organised compulsion.

At the "Labour" they told me I was a year too young to be given clerical work. "Could I join the Land Army?" I asked. Yes, I could, but I must be prepared to leave home. "That won't do, because my son is still at school." Very well, as you are a non-mobile woman, you have two alternatives left:

You can go into a factory; or

You can go into transport.

I thought of the heat, noise, electric light and airlessness of a munition factory and then I thought of the fresh air that blows from the Yorkshire moors across a tramcar platform in my city. And so I became a clippie – a tram conductress." [pp.5/6]

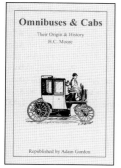

Omnibuses and Cabs – their Origin & History

H.C. Moore, reprint of 1901 publication, hardback, green cloth, dust wrapper, 282pp, 31 illustrations, £25

12 chapters devoted to omnibuses, from their origins in Paris in 1662. 2 chapters devoted to the rise and fall of Shillibeer. Other topics: the steam omnibus, the equirotal omnibus, Thomas Tilling, London General Omnibus Company, London Road Car Company, an electric omnibus, the well- conducted conductor and the ill-conducted conductor, fat and thin passengers, skid-men, ticket systems, the "corridor 'bus", "Jumpers", "Spots", pirate omnibuses - their history and tricks, etc.

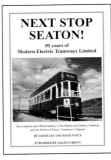

Next Stop Seaton

David Jay & David Voice, B5. softback, 140pp inc. covers, £17

Subtitled "50 years of Modern Electric Tramways Limited, the complete and official history of the Seaton and District Tramway and the Modern Electric Tramways Company".

"...the full story is told, often in great detail, from the early years with temporary installations, the short period at St. Leonards'-on-Sea to the more permanent homes at Eastbourne, and latterly Seaton. The illustrations throughout are superb, and appropriately illustrate the text. The section describing tramcars is comprehensive: every car is fully described with technical information and an illustration. Despite the wealth of information included the book is most readable, and is produced to the superb standards we have come to expect from Adam Gordon. Well worth buying, and a fitting tribute to 50 years of effort." [The Journal of the Tramway Museum Society].

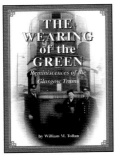

The Wearing of the Green

William Tollan. Softback, A4 size, 96 pages, 64 pages in mono, 16 pages in colour; covers coloured on both sides, £12

This describes the Glasgow tramways from c.1928-1951 from the viewpoint of a driver and conductor. "I think this is the most fascinating and amusing book on trams I have ever read." [Publisher]

"This is a dangerous book. Dangerous because once you pick it up you will find it impossible to put down until the end! ... Excellent value for money and thoroughly recommended." [Industrial Heritage]

"The book recalls the day when the tram reigned supreme over most of Clydesdale; it is well illustrated and appendices include extracts from traffic circulars and a full list of fare stages and a glossary. You will enjoy this book and even find the English translation of Auchenshuggle. [Tramway Review] "...well laid out and the pictures are crisply reproduced ... well worth reading by anyone who likes the social side rather than the history and minutiae." [Archive]

The Chateau Story

Elizabeth Varley. Softback, squareish format. 64pp; £10

The second non-transport book in this catalogue. She has written two other books: Mud on My Nylons (1950), and No More Champagne (1952). This is a mainly animal "fairy-tale", set in France long ago in the reign of a King Louis; described as "a children's story for grown-ups, or a grown-up's story for children" (so an ideal gift for any age!); 28 short chapters; principal animals are bears, squirrels, hedgehogs and mice, plus some spidery "Bush-Bushes"; 13 delightful full-page illustrations in colour, with many other tailpieces and decorative features by Lydia Nicholson.

[Elizabeth Varley is the mother of Adam Gordon]

Postage and packing on new books, UK retail: please add 10% of the value of the order up to £4.90 maximum. Orders £50 and over post free. Overseas postage extra, at cost. Overseas payments must please be by cheque, drawn on a British bank, and payable in Sterling or via bank-to-bank transfer.

ADAM GORDON, Kintradwell Farmhouse, Brora, Sutherland KW9 6LU.
Tel: 01408 622660   E-mail: adam@adamgordon.freewire.co.uk